Pewter Wares
from
Sheffield

Pewter Wares from Sheffield

JACK L. SCOTT

ANTIQUARY PRESS

BALTIMORE

PEWTER WARES FROM SHEFFIELD

Libarary of Congress Catalog Card Number: 80-68670
ISBN: 0-937864-00-5

PRINTED AND BOUND IN THE U.S.A.

ANTIQUARY PRESS
P.O. Box 9523
Baltimore, Md. 21237

To my love. . .

CONTENTS

PREFACE

This book had academic beginnings and, until a few weeks before this manuscript was happily sent up to the publisher, the title was, and had been from the beginning, *Britannia Metal and Pewter Wares from Sheffield.*

The purpose was to provide a scholarly history of the Britannia metal industry. The title seemed appropriate enough, for the wares produced in the 19th century were identified as Britannia metal, while the same exact products after World War I were called pewter. Hence the use of Britannia metal *and* pewter.

As the book developed, a much more practical purpose appeared. It then seemed that after spending some length in the Introduction explaining that Britannia metal is pewter, and that modern pewter is Britannia metal, coupled with the fact that Americans commonly refer to antique Britannia metal wares as pewter, concern arose that the original title would only confuse the issue.

So, in the interest of simplicity and practicality, the title was shortened at the last minute to its present form.

Writing the history of the Sheffield Britannia metal-pewter industry has been an exciting endeavor, for nearly everything in the research involved original sources.

Having a background in research and being an avid collector as well as a shop owner and dealer, I've tried to incorporate ideas which would be satisfying to others who have those individual or collective interests. At the same time, having read endless volumes of reference books on antiques, many of which have very little to say, well formed opinions developed in my mind concerning information that should be included in a useful reference. Likewise, opinions also have been formed relative to that which should be avoided in a good reference.

The historical aspect of the research proved to be necessary in providing the proper background to the industry and the goods which are now collected, bought, and sold as antique.

A great effort has also been made to keep the book functional, permitting collectors and dealers to get directly to the subject, What is it? Who made it? When? and Where?

One cannot seem to avoid the appearance of pet peeves when reading descriptive articles about antiques. A frequent annoyance is the use of the undated terms *early* and *late*. Many of us who read do so because we lack knowledge in an area. When the author describes an item as being "early" the term to the uninformed is not only meaningless, it is frustrating. The indefiniteness only leads to the questions how early and early in relation to what—the pyramids?! It also raises the possibility in the reader's mind that the author does not know the approximate age or date of the item and this can be unsettling.

A special effort has been made in this text to date each and every illustrated item, providing the reader with specific data.

A second peeve is the use of strong opinions as to taste or esthetic value, such as "attractive", "ugly", "lovely", "stunning", etc. One only has to look at the endless varieties of life to realize the truth of "beauty lies in the eyes of the beholder". Twenty years ago Victorian furniture was described in most uncomplimentary terms, yet, in two decades, the style has become quite the vogue.

The omission of descriptive adjectives has a purpose in the hope that readers may find their own personal satisfaction in the goods discovered from past years.

The reader may find some repetition of basic facts from one chapter to another and apologies are offered for these but they, too, have purpose. The text is basically a reference book which, in use, may never be read from cover to cover. Users will find it convenient to turn directly to the section in which they have a specific interest. To omit relative information in a chapter because it had been mentioned in a different section would be unfair to an inquiry in that chapter.

The dates given throughout the text and particularly in the chapter on maker's marks have been given every possible examination for accuracy. It is very easy in research to look up a company name in the city directory, note when the name first appears and then disappears, and enter these dates as the dates of operation or existence of the firm. But that is sloppy and often very inaccurate research. Old directories were a source of advertising and many firms did not participate at various times, or at all. Tax rolls, while more difficult to research, are much more reliable for everyone had to pay taxes. The rate (tax) books in Sheffield have been carefully examined to confirm or extend dates given by the directories.

Dated patent and design registrations have also been helpful. Newspaper articles, obituaries and advertisements, private sources and examples of wares were all blended together to pinpoint dates. Curiously, personal recollections are the least reliable of all sources. As a rule, at least three cross references have been examined to establish working dates for each maker.

The examples of goods used for illustration were for all practical purposes everything that could be found and photographed. Most are or have been in my own collection, while quite a few have passed through Hatt-In-Hand Antiques, the shop that my wife, Jan, and I own and enjoy.

The section in Chapter VIII on the makers and their marks varies slightly from the usual alphabetical sequence. In the instance of family surnames, the entries are listed in chronological order rather than alphabetical order by first name. This permits the users to see clearly the history of the firm from beginning to end.

4

Obviously, no one person can write a book without help, and, in my case, plenty of help. Jan has been a morale booster from the beginning. Her encouragement has made the work seem easy. I am deeply indebted to many people for their generous gifts of time and talents. Christine Markham and Julie MacDonald of Sheffield have been most helpful with their meticulous work for me in that city. Alvin Hoffman of Edgewood, Maryland, is responsible for the beautiful art work, including all the maker's marks. Alan Anderson of Anderson Photography, Bel Air, Maryland, not only took and processed all the photographs, he often had to travel many miles on very short notice to take a single picture. For editing and proof reading, I am grateful for the assistance given by Josephine Yingling of Bel Air, Maryland. To these friends, I give much thanks.

Jack L. Scott
Aberdeen, Maryland
October 15, 1980

INTRODUCTION

Sheffield pewter wares made, sold and used under the original trade description of Britannia metal seem to be the least understood and most frequently misrepresented of all 19th century goods now accepted as antique. The reason for this strange phenomenon is even now not clearly understood, for the wares were an important part of everyday life in the past century. Their design was typical of the period, and other goods of those times have enjoyed popularity with antiquarians. The Pewter Society of Great Britain accepts that Britannia metal is pewter but has a tendency to describe the wares made by casting the metal as pewter and those made of sheet stock specifically as Britannia metal wares.

In America the traditional feeling is that all wares of tin alloy are pewter. The American definition—

BRITANNIA METAL—A trade description originated in 1790 for many of the pewter wares produced in the late 18th century, 19th century and early 20th century.

One reason for a lack of interest has been the negative statements made by Cotterell in his book *Old Pewter, It's Makers and Marks*,[1] first published in 1929, and its subsequent reprints. Nearly everyone writing about English pewter since then has carried forth variations of those unfortunate remarks about Britannia metal.

The most valid reason of all may be that nothing of substance has been written about the English Britannia metal trade. One can find books, in some instances, a great many of them, on nearly all other products of the 19th century. These references give the backgrounds, makers' marks, dates, illustrations of their wares—all things that stimulate interest. Until now, no one had taken the time to research the Britannia metal industry.

The one short, but complimentary, chapter written by Bradbury as an appendage to *Old Sheffield Plate*,[2] is the only original writing that has been widely published about the Sheffield Britannia industry. The occasional articles, other than those written for *Spinning Wheel*[3] by this writer, have been gleaned from Bradbury's short chapter or were created with benefit of research.

1. Howard Herschell Cotterell, *Old Pewter, It's Makers and Marks*, London, 1929.
2. Frederick Bradbury, *History of Old Sheffield Plate*, Sheffield, 1912.
3. Jack L Scott, "Britannia Metal, A New Perspective", *Spinning Wheel*, March, April, May, June, 1973.

"Is it Pewter?" is the most frequently asked question concerning Britannia metal. The answer is clearly *yes*. Britannia metal *is* pewter. The chapters on the history of the industry, methods of construction and characteristic features answer all doubts in detail. A summary is given here as an introduction.

From a metallurgical point of view, there is no scientific or official alloy or formula for pewter. Pewter is a romantic term given by English-speaking people to products made of a high tin content alloy. These products probably should be called tin as they are in other countries such as Germany (*zinn*) and France (*e'tain*). Unfortunately, the English-speaking people use the word tim for products made of iron or steel and coated with tin, such as tin cans.

The formula for pewter has always varied greatly. While the basic ingredient has been tin, usually in the proportion of eighty to ninety-five percent, the remaining percentage of metal has varied in substance and quantity.

Bradbury states that of all samples analyzed for him, none contained the same proportions. Christopher Peal, England's contemporary authority on English pewter, reaffirms the wide variety of pewter alloys and confirms the use of antimony in the 18th century. He found the extremes of their proportions to be (in percentage) Tin 61-98, Lead 0-37, Antimony 0-5, Copper 0-3, and Bismuth 0-.05.[4] Those who feel that true pewter must contain lead in addition to the tin are on thin ice in several areas. Some very early and desirable pewter of the 15th century was made from a formula of tin and brass or copper—no lead. A great many of the 18th century traditional pewterers turned to the replacement of lead with antimony in order to produce a harder pewter. Additionally, all fine modern pewter wares are lead free.

A point to be made is that antiques are collected and used because they represent a certain period in time now long past. The exact formula for making ironstone china has never been a question among collectors of earthenwares, even though the product was made with different formulas and much was shipped to America under the trade description of Granite Ware. Why then, have pewter collectors dwelt on the issue of the formula?

Nearly all of the cast items made by the traditional 18th century pewterers continued to be cast in the same way by the 19th century Britannia metal makers. These makers additionally developed a wide range of new goods with methods borrowed from the silver trade.

It is incredible that pre-Victorian cast measures made and marked by DIXON & SON or I. VICKERS are passed up in favor of Edwardian, George V and even George VI measures because the Dixon and Vickers wares were "not pewter". Many collectors display pewter tankards and measures by Gaskell & Chambers of Birmingham, not knowing that these are basically 20th century products. Gaskell & Chambers organized in 1895 and is still active in Birmingham at present (1980). It is unfortunate that Cotterell gives the erroneous date for Gaskell & Chambers as c. 1840.

4. Christopher A. Peal, "Pewter In the 18th Century", *The Antique Dealer & Collectors Guide*, London, March, 1977.

Admittedly, the Britannia metal makers seldom referred to their products as pewter until the 20th century, but many 18th and 19th century traditional pewterers referred to their pewter by other names also, such as: *Hard White Metal, Best French Metal, Super Fine Metal,* etc.

For those who would demand more explicit proof that Britannia metal is pewter, reference should be made to Dr. Ernest S. Hedges, Director, International Tin Research Institute. Dr. Hedges, in *Tin And Its Alloys,*[5] correctly points out that modern pewter such as that produced in Sheffield and Birmingham from the early years of the 20th century and often referred to as lead-free pewter is exactly the same as Britannia metal.

It would seem obvious then, that the opposite would be equally true. If modern lead-free pewter is in fact Britannia metal, then Britannia metal must be pewter. The addition of new manufacturing techniques only served to improve an existing product and expand its possibilities. Britannia metal is a high-quality pewter which allows expanded functional usage.

5. Ernest S. Hedges, *Tin And Its Alloys*, London, 1960.

CHAPTER ONE
Sheffield
City of Metals

Sheffield is a wonderful city with a near perfect blend of the old and the new. The very center of the city features wide streets, modern shops, a new theater for dramatic arts and a unique underground round-about with an open center, where pedestrian shoppers can cross the street underground and window shop while on their way.

On the hills surrounding the city, modern housing innovations have drawn world wide attention. The smoke and smog which once characterized Sheffield is now gone, thanks to smokeless fuels.

Yet, with all the modern touches, Sheffield has not lost the character of historic past years. Municipal business is conducted in a magnificent Town Hall of obvious Victorian gothic style which opened with ceremonies attended by the Queen in 1897. Not far from the Town Hall is St. Peters Cathedral, one of the smallest cathedrals known; the nave of the church dating from the 15th century.

Fig. 1—**South-east view of Sheffield, 1858.** *Sheffield Central Library*

Fig. 2 — Recent View — Fargate St., Sheffield showing the Gothic Victorian tower of the Town Hall in the background. *Sheffield Central Library.*

16

Fig. 3—The round-about in the center of modern Sheffield not only allows free flow of traffic, but also features underground pedestrian walkways where walkers can window shop. *Sheffield Central Library*

Within the distance of a few blocks, one literally can walk into the past history of Sheffield's cutlery and allied trades. Craftsmen in small shops can still be found carrying out the trade that has for centuries made Sheffield synonymous with quality metal work. While it is true that most of the cutlery trade involves large factories, the concept of the small cubicle or shop stall has not completely died out, particularly in the instances of repairs and work involving specialty items such as handles or repair parts.

The ancient town was originally known as Escafeld, now Ecclesfield, and was a subdivision of Hallam. Later the town became known as Sheaffield and eventually Sheffield, taking it's name from the river Sheaf which converges with the river Don near the city center.

A castle was built at the junction of the Don and the Sheaf in the 12th century. The location of the castle and the eventual site of the church caused a shift of population and town center away from Ecclesfield to its present location, near the site of the old castle. The castle was the home of the Earl of Shrewsbury who was responsible for the confinement of Mary, Queen of Scots, from c. 1568 to c. 1584. The castle was destroyed by Parliament forces in 1644.

The Company of Cutlers was incorporated in 1624 and still functions today. The powers of the company originally included tight control of the quality of goods produced by all the cutlers within its six mile jurisdiction.

Many unique and important innovations relative to the metal trade had origins in Sheffield. About 1740, Benjamin Huntsman began experiments which

17

led to crucible steel, a steel harder and more even than that produced by smelting and forging. In 1743, Thomas Boulsover discovered the fusion of silver to copper which initiated the beginning of the tremendous Sheffield Plate trade. James Vickers began making wares of white metal in 1769 in Sheffield, and started an industry that grew to even greater proportions than the Sheffield Plate trade.

Although the process of electro plating of silver was invented and patented by two Elkington cousins from Birmingham, the first significant commercial application of the process occurred in Sheffield in 1843. From that year Sheffield maintained leadership in quality electroplated wares although eventually out-produced by Birmingham in total production volume.

Fig. 4 **Sheffield is well known for its many pleasant and spacious parks.** *Sheffield Central Library.*

In 1856, Henry Bessemer established large steel works in Sheffield utilizing his newly discovered methods for producing a good grade of steel in large quantities. The availability of steel was a boon to rapid industrial growth including the expansion of railroads.

Contrary to what would seem to be logical, the bulk of the iron used for the vast industries in Sheffield throughout the 18th and 19th centuries was not local, but came from Sweden and Russia. Very little use was made of English ores which were thought to be unsatisfactory. It was John Brown, later Sir John, who developed the use of domestic ores. Brown produced world famous armor plates for war ships in the city of metals.

One of three men working independently on the concept of a non-corrosive steel was Harry Brearley of Sheffield, who introduced stainless steel during the years 1912-1914.

Points of interest in Sheffield include the City Hall, built in 1932 for concerts; the City Museum, which houses an extensive collection of Sheffield Plate, Britannia metal and Derbyshire antiquities; the Central Library, noted for scientific references and local archives; the Graves Art Gallery; the Crucible, Sheffield's new theater; the Town Hall; Cutler's Hall; and St. Peter's Cathedral.

Mention should also be made of the University of Sheffield, the origin of which dates back to the founding of the medical school in 1828. Eventually Firth College was founded in 1879 and was chartered as the University of Sheffield in 1905, with King Edward VII attending the ceremonies. The University quickly assumed a rightful position among the other English Universities and has made signigicant contributions in the areas of metallurgy and glass technology. Not limited to the scientific, the University is known for its modern concepts and innovations in many areas including teacher education.

Fig. 5 **In addition to the original Edwardian buildings, the University of Sheffield features a modern high rise classroom building and library.**

The western end of the city looks out over the purple moors and wooded dales of Derbyshire. Sheffield is a spectacular sight at night, particularly when approaching the city from Derbyshire. The golden street lights and the new high rise housing on the opposite hills produce a fantasyland effect that is breathtaking.

Sheffield is also noted for its parks which are large and beautiful. The botanical gardens are at their highest glory in spring. Even the Peace Garden, a small park located downtown next to the Town Hall, is a welcome relief from the center of town activities.

In discussing the beautiful things about Sheffield, one cannot overlook the people of the city who are not only warm and friendly, but also express an unusual depth of sincerity. As is ever the instance with the local populace anywhere, most citizens are not aware of the wealth of history and significance that surrounds them in their home city. Perhaps this is desirable if it is a factor in producing such fine people in a city of history.

Fig. 6 Sheffield blends the old and the new. This view shows the University of Sheffield in the center with the original Edwardian buildings flanked by the recent modern additions. In the background can be seen modern high rise apartments. Intermingled are centuries old buildings. James Vickers began the Britannia metal industry in 1769, just a few blocks from the site of the present university. *Sheffield Central Library.*

CHAPTER TWO
History
of the Industry

Pewter is known to have been used in Britain by the Romans during their occupation. Some evidence suggests that a portion of the Roman pewter was made of local ores. Examples of their work are to be found in the British Museum and other collections.

Following the conclusion of Roman occupation, little is known of the use of pewter in Britain until the Middle Ages. The main vessels for eating and drinking during the early centuries of those dark times were made almost exclusively of wood. Forks were not known and the iron knife, being the chief tool for eating, often was the only non-wooden item at the table. Cotterell has indicated that after the Roman period no mention of pewter can be found in England until the 11th century, when an ordinance of the council of Worchester required that the chalices of poor parishes be made of pewter to replace the wooden ones then in use.

First appearing on the church altar and the table of nobility, pewter gradually became available for others as well. With the progression of years, those of the lower stations of life were slowly replacing their wooden trenchers and cups for those of pewter. The wealthy, by the 17th century, were replacing their pewter with imported porcelain from China. By mid-18th century the production of earthenwares and porcelains of the English potteries began to receive increased acceptance. The English goods were often produced in imitation of Chinese wares, hence the general term "china", referring to plates, dishes and other tableware.

The first quarter of the 18th century saw the beginning of economic and social growth which was to have a far reaching impact on England and the world. The wealthy class grew as did the merchant class, which eventually became the new middle class. This development of wealth is particularly evidenced by the tasteful Queen Ann designs now sought after by the 20th century connoisseur. By early 19th century the Industrial Revolution had given cities and towns not only a middle class, but a working class as well, each with buying power, even if limited in the instance of the working class.

As buying power increased, the potters turned out great quantities of wares aimed at all levels of society. The market turned to the Staffordshire and other potteries for the colorful and relatively inexpensive "china". As a result, the long established traditional pewter industry went into decline.

Silver remained out of reach of the middle class and most likely out of the fondest dreams of the working class, yet their enlightenment and desire for better things created a new market which was satisfied by two closely related Sheffield industries—the making of Sheffield Plate and Britannia metal wares.

In 1743, the method of plating silver on copper by fusion, now known as Old Sheffield Plate, was discovered in Sheffield by Thomas Boulsover. By 1750, an industry had begun that not only grew and flourished for one hundred years, but left an influence on style and design that has never completely fallen into disuse.

Sheffield Plate was a method of fusing silver on copper ingots by intense heat. The ingots were then processed through rollers until sheets of the desired thickness were obtained. Generally the sheets were plated on both sides, but in the very early years (1750-1755) and in the later years (1820-1845, for reasons of economy) the copper was plated on one side only, the reverse side being coated with tin to hide the copper.

These plated sheets were cut into parts, stamped or hand formed into shapes, assembled by soldering, and made into tea wares and hundreds of domestic items. The goods were made up in the same manner as those of solid silver with one notable exception. The edges left the copper center exposed. This brought about the unique feature of Sheffield Plate—borders, edges and decoration were added to cover the exposed copper. By the first quarter of the 19th century, these decorations had become quite elaborate and were an established feature of the industry. The goods could not be distinguished from those made of sterling except by the absence of official hall marks or very close and knowledgeable inspection. The cost of these wares averaged just a little more than half the cost of those in solid silver.

In spite of the wars with the American Colonies, France and Spain, towards the end of the 18th century and into the 19th century, the Industrial Revolution moved ahead, increasing economic growth. Public expenditure in England rose from £27,500,000 in 1792, to £173,500,000 in 1815. The new prosperity continued to bring greater social awareness.

Wealthy families continued to buy silver and fine porcelain, while the emerging middle class purchased the very stylish Sheffield Plate and colorful earthenwares. Taking tea became very social and by the end of the 18th century, "tea" had become an establishment in its own right.

The middle class and the less prosperous working class also looked for a product which would add a touch of elegance or finery to their home life. This economic market was one factor which prepared the way for the Britannia metal industry. The question has been raised as to why the long established pewterers could not supply the need for elaborate tea services and tableware at modest cost. Unfortunately, by the end of the 18th century, the pewter industry had been reduced to the limited production of plates, tankards and measures. Collectors of 18th century traditional pewter will point to many exceptions to the previous statement, but that is exactly what they are—exceptions. Late 18th century trade cards of London pewterers clearly illustrate teapots, cannisters, cream jugs and other related items, yet few of these were made in London and it was left to the Sheffield men to produce the goods in quantity.

The logical question is "Why?" The established pewterers recognized the market potential but couldn't produce the goods. The concept of pewter making had always been exclusively one of casting. All parts were cast in moulds, then soldered together and finished on a lathe or by hand. The investment in very expensive moulds for new products in a declining industry proved to be too speculative. Of greater importance was the fact that casting produced a thick and heavy product which did not provide the feeling of elegance which the market demanded.

A new metal product designed for the lower social classes was envisioned by two men in two different metal working cities, coincidently in the same year.

It was in 1769 that William Tutin of Birmingham began to experiment with a new metal for casting buckles and spoons. His formula consisted of eight parts brass, thirty-two parts antimony and seven part tin. Tutin patented his new metal, called Tutania, in 1770, and several Birmingham makers made spoons and buckles of Tutania. Shoe buckles went out of style at the turn of the century but the inventor made spoons of Tutania until 1825, and spoons continued to be made of the patented metal until 1839, when the last entry for Tutania is found in the Birmingham directories. Two final makers are listed for that year, A. Hill & Son and John Yates, whose name is well known to collectors of 19th century English pewter spoons and ladles.

Although Tutania spoons were made for seventy years in Birmingham, production remained limited, sharing the market with spoons made of iron, brass, tinned iron, pewter, and, from about 1826, nickle silver. Tutania had very little impact, primarily because it was a cast metal of limited use which had to compete with items cast in the same manner as other metals.

It was in the same year, 1769, that James Vickers took up residence and shop on Hollis Street in Sheffield, amidst a large colony of silversmiths and platers, the pewter industry being unknown in Sheffield at that time. This date is given in a traditional story related by Charles Dixon, an early 19th century manufacturer and amateur historian from Sheffield.

> About the year 1769, a person was taken very
> ill, and Mr. Vickers visited him in his sickness.
> This person was in possession of the recipe for
> making white metal. Mr. Vickers bid him five
> shillings for the recipe, and the offer was
> accepted.

The "recipe" purchased by Vickers was essentially the same as that used by the London makers for their best wares.

This date is further confirmed by the fact that James Vickers first appears in the Sheffield rate (tax) books for that year. Dixon's story also relates that Vickers borrowed ten pounds sterling to make his first items, which were cast spoons. He took the spoons, made with borrowed capital, to London where they were well received and quickly sold. From this modest beginning of a few spoons successfully marketed in London, rose the vast pewter industry in which the wares were known as Britannia metal in the 19th century and lead free pewter in the 20th century.

The relationship between the wares which were to become known as

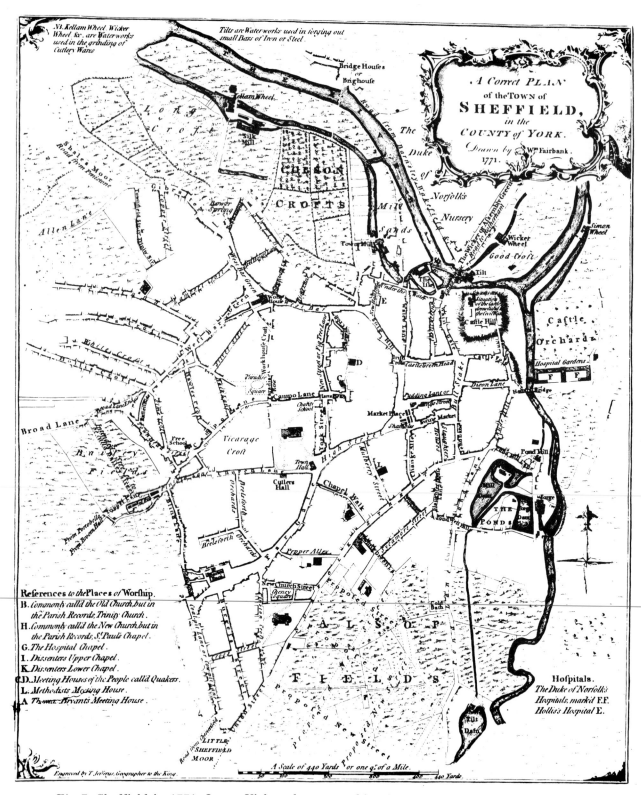

Fig. 7 Sheffield in 1771. James Vickers began working in Hollis Croft (left center) in 1769. *Sheffield Central Library.*

26

Britannia metal and those produced by the earlier pewterers may be much closer than here-to-fore realized. Wares in the 17th and 18th centuries were made of either common pewter or a better quality hard metal often known as Superfine *White Metal*. These hard or white metal wares were also described as *French Pewter*, the reason for which is given later in the chapter. Until recently, the difference between common and hard metal wares was generally assumed to be simply the variation in the lead content of the alloy.

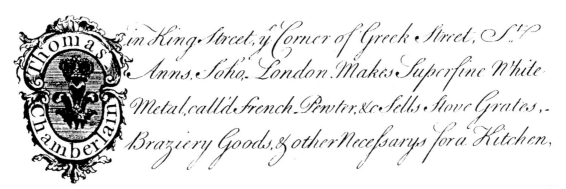

Fig. 8 **A trade card of Thomas Chamberlain (1734-c.1776), showing the mid 18th century use of white metal in London.** *Copyright British Museum.*

In the interest of scientific accuracy, The Worshipful Company of Pewterers recently contributed 17th, 18th, and early 19th century wares for sophisticated modern analysis. The results show two revealing, if not startling facts. The pewterers had been secretely adding significant amounts of antimony to their best metal and in the 18th century particularly, the lead in the best wares was so negligible that it was certainly not an additive, but an accidental impurity in the tin. The 18th century wares consisted on an average of 96% tin, 3.2% antimony, .5% copper and small traces of silver, zinc and lead. While the 17th century makers added an average of 1.5% copper, it had become just a trace in the following century, only to be generally revived to the 1.5 to 2% level in the 19th century.

There was, of course, no standard formula for pewter. Wares of this metal should rightly be called *tin* using the analogy that all products of gold alloy, even at nine karat (37.5%) are known as *gold*. The basic and dominant ingredient of pewter has always been tin and over the centuries additives have included brass, copper, lead, antimony, zinc, bismuth and even aluminum. These secondary metals have been added for one or more reasons; (1) to make the products cheaper, (2) to make the metal harder, (3) to facilitate fabrication into wares.

Vickers, surrounded everywhere in Sheffield with rolling mills and sheet metal, very quickly applied the rolling principle with the discovery that his white metal was very well suited for rolling into sheet stock. Utilizing the resources, knowledge, work skills, available rolling mills, stamps, dies, engravers and techniques allied to the silver and plated trades, Vickers began to make products in white metal in the same manner and style as the silversmiths and platers. These early white metal products were copies of items made in silver and plate. They were sold, of course, at a substantially lower cost than the products which they copied. The market was then covered. The buying public had a complete choice of products and cost: silver, Sheffield Plate and white metal.

From the very beginning of the trade, emphasis was placed on craftsmanship and quality as well as good design. The range of goods made by Vickers during the first years is not known, but his advertisement in the directory for 1787 is interesting.

BITS and STIRRUPS.

Vickers James, Garden Walk, *plated with White Metal.*
(He makes alſo Meaſures, Tea Pots, Caſtor Frames,
Salts, Spoons, &c. of the ſame Metal).

The announcement seems to emphasize the fact that he plated bits and stirrups with white metal, yet the added note, *"He makes also measures, teapots, castor frames, salts, spoons, etc."* gives a very strong clue that in eighteen years his variety of goods was rather extensive. Vickers, unlike the London makers, did not make all sorts of pewter, but produced best quality white metal wares exclusively. Living in a community of silversmiths he quickly became known as a white metalsmith.

Little information is available on the life of James Vickers, but it is generally known that he was a humble man who drew the respect of his fellow citizens even though he was a Methodist at a time when being a dissenter was particuarly unpopular.

Vickers' wife was the daughter of Thomas Holy, a Sheffield silversmith. The Vickers joined the Methodist Society in 1763. By 1792, their son, John, was active in the business. Vickers was prominent in Methodist affairs at the chapel on Garden Street, the same street where he lived and worked. He became involved in community affairs and in 1793 was appointed Overseer of the Poor. In 1797 he was made a constable. James Vickers died in 1809 and the business continued under the direction of his son.

The first person to enter the trade following James Vickers is unknown, but an obituary of 1813 states that Nathanial Gower entered the white metal trade some forty years earlier (1773) with G. Smith as a partner. The business was short lived and Gower moved into the plated trade. By 1785, several cutlers were using white metal in the production of handles for steel knives and William Holdsworth began to make spoons in the same year. The Holdsworth family continued to make spoons exclusively until mid-19th century when a complete range of wares including electroplate were then produced. The directory for 1792 lists four makers in addition to Vickers. The rate books confirm that Richard Constantine began business in 1792. Hancock and Jessop were makers of Sheffield Plate who also made Britannia metal and their partnership dates from 1790. The other two firms were Broadhead, Gurney, Sporle & Co., and Froggatt, Coldwell & Lean, both of whom were manufacturers of Sheffield Plate and Britannia metal. Their partnerships date from about 1792. It is interesting to note that the three partnerships were very short lived. Henry Froggatt, however, continued in the trade for many years.

28

The contribution of James Vickers was not a new metal as had previously been thought, but the application of techniques new to the pewter industry. It should be noted that spinning was not used and did not appear in the industry until much later, about 1825.

Although the new products attracted wide attention, the makers also supplied spoons, pepper pots, salts, measures, etc., which were cast in moulds as had been done for many years by the earlier pewterers.

In 17th and 18th century London, pewter wares made of hard metal were often sold as "French pewter," the wares were, of course, not made in France, or made of metal from France. The origin of the term is attributed to James Taudin, a French Protestant refugee who settled in London during the 17th century. Taudin registered and used a touch mark which included the phrase E. SONNANT (ringing tin). The meaning, in English, became hard metal. In general, hard metal wares became known as French pewter. Many London pewterers used the term, which became synonymous with best quality hard white metal.

However, due to the political climate during the later decades of the century, anti-French feelings were very strong. About 1790 the crafty Sheffield makers devised their own trade description for white metal wares and in a stand for patriotism (commercially inspired) offered the public their Britannia metal in lieu of the French Pewter produced in London. The term Britannia metal remained a popular description well into the 20th century.

An interesting advertisement from the *Sheffield Courant* of June 14, 1796, tends to confirm the general feeling that Britannia metal was a better grade of pewter.

> *Two or three workman wanted in a Pewter Manufactory*
> *as spoonmakers viz. Queens Britannia and Common*
> *Pewter spoons.*

A second advertisement, appearing in the *Sheffield Iris* of May 10, 1799, shows that some tea wares were made in Sheffield on contract for London pewterers.

> *A good workman or two in the Britannia metal teapot,*
> *etc. line may meet with contract employ by applying to*
> *Towsend and Compton, London.*

The manufacture of Britannia metal goods remained exclusively a Sheffield industry during the 18th century, and by 1814 Sheffield boasted fifteen makers of Britannia metal wares. During the first decade of the 19th century, the production of the metal had begun in Birmingham where a substantial industry grew, although never equal to that of Sheffield. It is surprising that the successful use of antimony remained unknown in America until 1806,[1] where the industry had very few ties with Sheffield or Birmingham. The techniques and designs of the Americans were, for the greater part, uniquely their own.

The industry grew hand in hand with the plated trade. Large factories, utilizing steam and water power, employed hundreds of workers to turn out products of exceptional quality.

6. Katherine Ebert, *Collecting American Pewter*, New York, 1973.

It would seem that by the year 1825, nearly everything of a domestic nature which was made in Sheffield Plate was also made in Britannia metal with the exception of knives, forks and elaborate candelabra, which were not suited for construction in the softer Britannia metal.

Unfortunately, this knowledge of large factories often comes as a severe blow to the collector, who in cherishing a favorite item, had envisioned a little old craftsman alone at his small work shop making each and every article bearing his name. It is true that a large percentage of the work utilized hand craftsmanship, but much of the work received assistance from power machinery, and goods were turned out by hundreds of such craftsmen working for the factory owner whose name appears on the bottom of the articles. One can be reasonably assured that the three industries of silver, Sheffield Plate and Britannia metal, in most instances involved large productive factories. James Dixon had built a new factory for the manufacture of Britannia metal goods in 1822, and by 1846 there were four hundred employees at work there. With the passing of fifty additional years, the number of workers at this one factory had more than doubled.

Fig. 9 **The Philip Ashberry plant on Bowling Green Street. c. 1840.** *Sheffield Centray Library.*

SUPERIOR BRITANNIA METAL

BROADHEAD & ATKIN,
NORTH-STREET WORKS,
Sheffield,

Manufacturers, in Britannia Metal,

OF

TEA AND COFFEE POTS,
Improved Coffee Percolators,

SUGAR BASINS, CREAM EWERS, SPOONS, LADLES,

CANDLESTICKS, INKSTANDS,

ALE AND LIQUOR MEASURES,

Drinking Cups,

DISHES, PLATES AND COVERS, MOUNTED EARTHENWARE JUGS,

SERVICES, &c. &c.

————o————

The advantages of Britannia Goods being so universally known as to require no comment, B. & A. merely take upon themselves to state, that, where articles from their Establishment have once been introduced, they have given that satisfaction, which (they feel it their duty to observe) has caused a very increased demand for the general goods of their manufacture.

4*

Fig. 10 Broadhead & Akin advertisement of 1834, showing the wide range of goods produced. *Sheffield Central Library.*

Fig. 11 The R. Broadhead & Co. plant located on Love Street, c. 1855. The premises was originally occupied by Broadhead & Atkin in 1843. *Sheffield Central Library.*

In the early years of the 19th century, the Britannia metal manufacturers continued to duplicate the designs of earlier and contemporary silver and plate. Often the very same dies were used. As the Sheffield Plate designs became more and more ornate (c. 1830-1845) the most popular Britannia metal designs remained those of clean lines and traditional forms. Designs for coffee pots were often copies of George I and George II silver styles. The Britannia metal trade unknowingly continued the long standing tradition of the earlier English pewterers of producing wares of good taste, fine proportions and simple lines.

The industry grew in production volume, although there were only thirteen firms in Sheffield during the years of 1842-1845, when extraordinary events took place in Birmingham and Sheffield which had a profound effect on the industry.

On September 25, 1840, Elkington's of Birmingham was granted patent No. 8447 for electroplating silver onto a base metal. This patent was preceded by less definitive patents and followed by improvement patents, but Leader[7] considered the 1840 patent to be the master patent for electroplating.

7. R. E. Leader, *The Early History of Electro-Silver Plating*, London, 1919.

After a successful three year fight to protect their process, the patentees set about to find manufactureres who would use the process on license from the inventors. Their first approach was to the Sheffield Platers, but the great old firms who had been successful at producing fused plated goods would not accept the new process. Elkington's then turned to the Britannia metal trade, who accepted the concept of electroplating as a sound business move. The original purpose of Britannia metal had been to provide a substitute for silver and Sheffield Plate and the electroplating process brought them closer to their original intent. Britannia metal plated very well and required no changes in production other than adding the plating process.

Although three minor licenses had been granted early in 1843, one to a London firm, the other two in Birmingham, the first major license to produce electroplated wares was granted to the well established Britannia metal firm owned by John Harrison in Sheffield. The date was June 13, 1843. The very next day a license was granted to W. C. Hutton, of Sheffield, and from that date the number of Britannia metal firms in Sheffield who would become electroplaters continued to grow until the figure neared the one hundred mark at the end of the century.

The license concept lasted only a few years and Elkington's was unable to keep control of the rapidly expanding industry. Most manufactureres soon took up the process without bothering to secure a license or to pay royalties to the inventors.

The end result was that by 1850 the Sheffield Plate Industry was, for all practical purposes, finished. Only three long established firms continued to make goods and those were a very limited production, mainly for the hotel and tavern trade.

Adding the electroplate market to the already established Britannia metal market, coupled with general economic growth and expansion of the Empire, meant continued prosperity for the Sheffield manufacturers.

By 1883 there were ninety-nine factories in Sheffield producing a general line of plated and Britannia metal goods. This figure does not include many small firms which produced specialty items such as spoons, buttons and cutlery accessories. James Dixon & Sons was one of the leading firms during this period and employed some nine hundred men and women in the factory.

The market for Britannia metal slipped into a slow but steady decline beginning about 1870, as the plated trade replaced more and more of the market and Britannia metal simply went out of vogue.

Strangely enough, it was prosperity which gave Britannia metal such a bad name in the late 19th and early 20th centuries. It is unfortunate that this undeserved reputation has lingered on to the present time.

Ornate designs with vines, leaves, flowers, heavy embossment, machine stamped "engraving" and many hurried and non-traditional shapes and designs were developed in the electroplate factories to satisfy an every growing public who continuously wanted something new and different. These "Victorian" wares were electroplated over a base of Britannia metal. When new and brightly plated, the goods were thought to be attractive and desirable, but when well used and with the plating worn through to the Britannia metal, they became unattractive. Added to many designs of questionable merit were problems connected with competition for the market.

Unlike the early years of the 19th century, wages became an important cost factor in manufacturing. The Industrial Revolution brought social reform, which meant better wages for the workers and higher prices for the consumer.

In a continuing effort to keep prices competitive, many firms cheapened their product. This was particularly true of the makers who sold unmarked goods. Cheap electroplated goods were made of a very thin gauge metal. They were often made with lead handles, feet and knobs, and lead weights were hidden inside the spouts to offset the lightness of the product. These goods received only the very lightest coating of silver.

Obviously this class of goods did not wear well. Many thousands of these low quality goods were put on the market during the period 1880-1914, although they were often marked E.P.B.M.,[8] many were not so designated and after the thin plating had worn completely away, the wares, which may still be found in abundance, were identified as "Britannia Metal". They were, in fact, Victorian electroplate. Nearly all the examples which have been thrust forward as being undesirable Britannia metal can be traced back to the electroplate trade.

Fig. 12 This sugar bowl of c. 1890 is a good example of cheap electroplated wares which when worn, shows the base metal of Britannia metal. It is this type of goods which brings undeserved, unkind and degrading reference to Britannia metal. The metal is paper thin and spun of one piece with a rolled edge. The handles and feet are lead (cheaper than Britannia) and the silver was the thinnest possible coating. Finally, the engraving is machine done. These obvious cheap goods were almost exclusively the product of the electroplated industry and not the Britannia metal trade. For the most part, they were made in manufacturing centers other than Sheffield.

8. Electro Plated Britannia Metal

It would be safe to say that the production of Britannia metal goods, unplated, and sold as unplated Britannia metal retained their quality, but declined steadily in production until 1914, when production stopped entirely with the beginning of World War I.

An interesting development which we call Art Nouveau occurred at the very end of the Victorian Age. One medium used during this short art period was pewter. Vases, bowls, personal items, jewelery and other items were formed in pewter, often set with colored glass stones. In most instances the metal used was Britannia metal, although these art forms and limited production items were said to be made of and are universally described as pewter. Hence we have one of the first instances of Britannia metal specifically and purposely being identified as pewter.

Following the Great War, radio, automobiles, airplanes and the modern age became a reality. It was a new world and suddenly the 19th century seemed very much in the past.

Hardly had England stepped into this new world when an interest in old pewter developed and, with it, an interest in new pewter. The interest in old pewter prompted the production of fakes and reproductions, many of which with passage of fifty years or more are now accepted in many collections as being authentic. It was the interest in old pewter which naturally led to an interest in a market for contemporary wares.

There were only nine firms that returned to the manufacture of Britannia metal goods after the war, all of which produced electroplated and sterling silver wares as their main line. These firms, along with those in Birmingham, developed new designs to meet the interest in pewter. Their wares were stamped BEST ENGLISH PEWTER. The metal was the same as it had always been.

Philip Ashberry & Sons was one of the first to change the name of its products from Birtannia metal to pewter. James Dixon & Sons, makers of Britannia metal since 1804, realized the market potential for goods sold as pewter in 1927 when they came out with their trade description "Cornish Pewter". George Lee & Co. had its beginning as William Brown, maker of Britannia metal wares in 1814, and about 1929 marked products as pewter under the name of MY LADY. Many other produced pewter wares under registered trade marks such as Don Pewter. Howard Pewter, Manor Period Pewter, etc. Modern pewter, or lead free pewter is in reality Britannia metal, just as 19th century Britannia is in reality, pewter.

The production of modern pewter continued until the start of World War II in 1939, when all the Sheffield firms converted to the war effort. One leading firm produced petrol drum covers and small munitions parts, while others made similar items.

After the war, recovery was a slow process for Sheffield which had been the target for enemy bombing. Production increased slowly but made dramatic strides starting in 1965 when Sheffield pewter products began to find a world wide market. In 1972 the number of firms producing pewter was eleven, all of which enjoyed a heavy export trade.

In 1974 one firm alone produced goods in excess of two million dollars, over one and a half million dollars of which was exported to the U.S.A.

The most popular item currently produced in Sheffield is no longer the teapot but the mug or tankard. However, a complete line of functional and decorative wares are produced for a world wide market.

The Britannia metal/pewter industry has been a staple factor in Sheffield's economy for over two hundred years. Goods made in Sheffield have reached all parts of the world and antique items are now important parts of extensive collections. Modern products are used and enjoyed everywhere. The success of the industry which was built on quality, craftsmanship and good design can be measured by the three hundred or more firms which have produced the wares, by the value of those goods produced annually down through the years, and by the longevity of so many of the firms.

Fig. 13 Contemporary Sheffield tankards are very popular in America where they are often given as awards and mementos. This young lady proudly displays a tankard, appropriately engraved, commemorating her award for having the best attendance in her high school band.

CHAPTER THREE
James Dixon

James Dixon

James Dixon was born in Sheffield early in the year of 1776, the records of the parish church showing the baptism date to be February 25, 1776. He was the son of James Dixon.[9] Like so many young lads in Sheffield, he grew up in a metal working family.

In 1790, at the age of 14, Dixon was apprenticed to Samuel Broadhead, a Sheffield Plate manufacturer, who, about 1792, became the senior partner in the firm Broadhead, Gurney, Sporle & Co. The firm manufactured Sheffield Plate and white metal goods and was the parent firm for Broadhead & Atkin which was organized in 1834. That firm subsequently became two separate companies in 1853, R. Broadhead & Co., which survived until 1900 and Atkin Brothers, which remained in business until 1957, both companies being typical examples of the continuity of manufacturing firms in Sheffield.

It was the general practice in the 18th and early 19th century for a lad to be apprenticed to a master for seven or more years. The apprentice usually lived with the master and his family, who provided for the young man while at the same time teaching him a trade. He received training, board and keep and token annual wages in exchange for working for the master while learning the trade. Writers have often depicted the apprenticed as being abused, exploited and over-worked, but such was not always the case. In many instances the relationship was more like father and son, as the apprentice literally became part of the master's family.

In 1797, the young Dixon, then 21 years of age, finished his apprenticeship and became a freeman. Like most who received no real pay while apprenticed, he had little if any funds available to start his own business. The only alternative was to seek employment as a journeyman. For the following seven or eight years, Dixon worked for Richard Constantine, a well known and important Britannia metal manufacturer. Wages were very low and it was difficult for Dixon to save from his earnings towards his ultimate goal of establishing his own business.

Finally, about the year 1804, James Dixon was able to begin his own business in the growing Britannia metal trade. The exact foundation date has not been established as there are no rate books or directories in existence for the years 1804-5-6. The notice of the death of James Willis Dixon in 1917 states the firm began in 1804, yet the centenary of the firm was celebrated in July of 1906.

9. The name James Dixon was frequently seen in Sheffield. In the year 1776 there also was a James Dixon, pocket knife cutler, and James Dixon, a vicar. A second infant James Dixon was also born in that same year.

There were six other established firms producing Britannia metal goods in Sheffield during the first decade of the 19th century. Dixon entered the business at a very opportune time, for the economic growth of England was escalating at a rapid rate. There is evidence which suggests that Dixon began on his own, taking Thomas Smith in as a partner in 1811. The rate books for 1807 through 1810-1811 list only James Dixon at 42 Silver Street, and Dixon and Smith from 1811-1812 through 1822. Bradbury gives a mark for early Dixon wares as simply DIXON. The use of the last name only for a mark is in keeping with practice in Sheffield during this period. This mark has not been confirmed with any known example, although examples marked DIXON & SMITH do exist.

The partnership was for certain in 1811, producing wares of very fine quality, including teawares, coffee pots, beakers, segar (sic) boxes, candlesticks, pap boats, tankards, snuff boxes, inkstands, egg cups, mustard pots, cruet sets, goblets, lidded beer jugs, tobacco jars, salts, communion wares, covered dishes, chambersticks, pepper pots, canteens, tea caddies, hot water dishes, dish covers, spoons and ladles. The simple mark used by Dixon & Smith[10] was occasionally accompanied by a small workman's number indicating by whom the object had been crafted. Items made by Dixon & Smith are a rare find for collectors, as are most products of the late Georgian-pre Victorian period.

The Dixon & Smith works were located in an area not far from the ancient parish church, now the cathedral. Silver Street is not of great length and the original buildings were torn down early in the present century for construction of a trolley barn.

10. All Dixon marks are given in chapter VIII.

Fig. 14 **The new Dixon Plant at Cornish Place, in 1822.**

In 1822, while maintaining production at Silver Street, new facilities were being built at Cornish Place on the River Don. The new factory was surrounded by "beautiful woodlands and green pastures", and the River Don was said to have been a salmon river of considerable importance. One innovative feature was the use of steam power for the operation of much of the equipment.

The partnership continued until the end of 1822 when Thomas Smith left the company and James Dixon took in his eldest son William Frederick Dixon as a partner. The firm then became DIXON & SON. At this point the facilities in Silver Street were given up and all production then originated at the new plant at Cornish Place. The greatly increased facilities led to a rapid expansion in production and sales, and within a few years heavy export to America had begun.

From 1823, an interesting indenture survives which apprenticed Joshua Biggin to James Dixon and William Frederick Dixon. The term of the indenture was a very unusual nine years and eight weeks and wages were 16 pence per year. Normally the apprentice lived with the master who supplied all his needs. According to the agreement between Biggin and the Dixons, Joshua, the apprentice, was to live at home and the father, John Biggin, was to be compensated seven shillings a week for the first two years and eight shillings a week for the remaining years of the contract. The payment was to cover the expense of "meat, drink, washing, lodging, and wearing apparel" for the lad. Joshua eventually served his apprenticeship with the Dixons and remained for many years in their employ as a journeyman and eventually as head of a department.

Unknowingly, King George IV gave a boost to the Britannia metal industry when he standardized liquid and bulk measures with the introduction of the Imperial measure in 1824.

Previously, the measure for wine was smaller than that for ale. The new Imperial measure standardized the gallon, quart, pint, gill and half gill to be the same for all liquids. Imperial measure was larger than the old wine or ale measure, hence new tankards and measures had to be made for all public houses and inns.

Dixon & Son, along with other Britannia metal firms, capitalized on the new law, producing large quantities of Imperial measures and tankards. Some measures were styled and cast in the exact same manner as the existing traditional pewter measures. Others were unique to Sheffield.

As the firm grew, so did the general line of goods which were centered around tea wares. New styles gave a greater variety of choice as well as relief from the canoe or boat shapes which had been so popular the previous twenty years. During the period 1823-1829, goods were marked DIXON & SON, but because styles and designs increased so greatly, pattern numbers were occasionally included on goods made during the latter two years. These goods, marked DIXON & SON with a three or four digit pattern number plus a workman's number, may be reasonably attributed to the years 1828-1829.

James Dixon had been continuously successful from the outset, but is was from 1829 that the greatest expansions and developments began to take place.

This Indenture

made the ___ Day of January ___

in the ___ Year of the Reign of our Sovereign Lord GEORGE the Fourth, by the Grace of God of the United Kingdom of *Great Britain* and *Ireland*, KING, Defender of the Faith, and in the Year of our LORD One Thousand Eight Hundred and Twenty Three ___ BETWEEN *John Biggin the son of John Biggin of Brightlin* ___ of the one Part and ___ *James Dean and William Fenton of Harris Oaks, Sheffield* ___

of the other Part; WITNESSETH, That the said *John Biggin* ___ hath of *his* own Free will, and with the Consent of ___ put and bound *himself* Apprentice to and with the said *James Dean and William Fenton* ___ *remain, and serve from* the ___ after the manner of an Apprentice, to ___ remain, and serve from the ___ Years thence next following be fully completed and ended; during all which Term, the said Apprentice *his* said Master ___ well and faithfully shall serve, *his* Secrets shall keep, *his* lawful Commands shall do, Fornication or Adultery shall not commit, Hurt or Damage to *his* said Master ___ shall not do, or consent to be done, but to the utmost of *his* power shall prevent it, and forthwith *his* said Master ___ thereof warn: Taverns or Ale-houses *he* ___ shall not haunt or frequent, unless it be about *his* Master's ___ Business there to be done: At Dice, Cards, Tables, Bowls, or any other unlawful Games *he* ___ shall not play: the Goods of *his* said Master ___ shall not waste nor them lend, or give to any Person without *his* said Master ___ Licence: Matrimony within the said Term shall not contract, nor from *his* said Master's ___ Service at any time absent *himself*; but as a true and faithful Apprentice shall order and behave *himself* towards *his* said Master ___ as well in Words as in Deeds during the said Term: And a true and just Account of all *his* said Master's ___ Goods, Chattels, and Money committed to *his* Charge, or which shall come to *his* Hands, faithfully *he* ___ shall give at all Times when thereunto required by *his* said Master ___ Executors, Administrators, or Assigns. AND the said *James Dean and William Fenton* ___

for themselves ___ Executors, Administrators, and Assigns, *do* covenant, promise, and agree *by these Presents*, to and with the said ___ Executors, Administrators, or Assigns, shall and will Apprentice, That *they* the said *James Dean and William Fenton* ___ teach, learn, and instruct *him*, the said Apprentice, or cause *him* to be taught, learned, and instructed in the Art or Mystery of a Manufacturer of Britannia Metal ___ Goods a Business ___ which the said Master ___ now use *th*, after the best manner that ___ *or* they may or can, with all Circumstances thereunto belonging: And also, ___ find and provide to and for ___ to the said Apprentice, sufficient and enough of Meat for Wages ___

And for the true performance of all and singular the Covenants and Agreements aforesaid, each of the Parties aforesaid doth bind himself unto the other firmly by these Presents. In Witness whereof, the Parties above-named to these present Indentures, interchangeably have set their Hands and Seals the Day and Year above-written.

Signed Sealed and Delivered, (being first duly stamped) by all the said Parties
in *the* presence of ___

Josiah Biggin

John Biggin

James Dean

W. F. Fenton

Dixon, from his early apprentice days, had always wanted to work in silver, and in 1829 registered as a silversmith with the Sheffield Assay Office. Sheffield Plate was added to production at that time, as he had purchased all the assets of the plating firm of Nicholson, Ashforth and Cutts. His first Sheffield Plate mark (which was not required to be registered) was registered with Cutlers Hall in 1835.

It was a busy and prosperous time for the Dixon factory. Hunting accessories were added to production. Powder and shot flasks in copper and brass, as well as wine flasks, shot, sandwich and cheese boxes, and other items related to hunting and shooting were also produced. The line of hunting goods continued to expand as the development of fire arms progressed, and by 1876 an extensive catalog of complete hunting accessories was offered by James Dixon & Sons.

Fig. 15 Two dixon powder flasks. The left is bronze copper with brass fittings, Mark No. 141 c. 1835. The right is leather covered with British Plate fittings and has a diamond registration mark for May 6, 1856, Mark No. 152.

A slight change occurred in the Dixon mark during the years 1830-1834. The word JAMES was added above the previous mark so that it read:

JAMES
DIXON & SON

A second son, James Willis Dixon, was taken in as a partner in 1835 and went to America as a traveller (sales representative). While in America he established four sales agencies for Dixon wares. A son, James Willis, Jr., was born in New York on September 16, 1838. The fast growing country with a need for manufactured goods provided an excellent market for the hunting accessories, Britannia metal goods, and elegant Sheffield Plate. More antique Dixon Britannia metal of the period 1825-1845 may be found in present day America than the combined production of all the American pewterers and Britannia metalsmiths of the same period.

With the addition of the second son to the partnership in 1835 the mark was accordingly changed to read:

JAMES
DIXON & SONS

44

JAMES DIXON AND SON,

CORNISH-PLACE, SHEFFIELD,

MANUFACTURERS OF

Superior Britannia Metal Goods,

WHICH,

FOR STYLE, VARIETY OF PATTERN, AND BRILLIANCY OF POLISH,

Combined with excellent Workmanship, stand unrivalled.

JAMES DIXON AND SON,

MANUFACTURERS OF SILVER GOODS,

OF THE NEWEST AND MOST SUPERB PATTERNS,

AND

RICH SHEFFIELD PLATED WARES,

With strong Silver Edges, and Shields,

UPON WHICH TO ENGRAVE ARMS AND CRESTS; WARRANTED OF THE MOST SUPERIOR AS WELL AS DURABLE QUALITY.

JAMES DIXON AND SON,

MANUFACTURERS OF

Bronze Copper Powder and Pistol Flasks,

LEATHER SHOT-POUCHES, BELTS,

GAME BAGS, &c. &c.

OF EXCELLENT WORKMANSHIP,

IN THE GREATEST VARIETY.

Fig. 16 James Dixon & Son advertisement of 1834. Sheffield Central Library.

This mark continued in use until Dixon's retirement in 1842. Eventually a third son, Henry Issac Dixon, and a son-in-law, William Fawcett, became full partners in the firm. Fawcett became mayor of Sheffield in 1855.

Artistic designers were employed to create new and distinctive patterns for Sheffield Plate and Britannia metal goods. Design and style became an important key as customers continually demanded something new. The many manufacturers all over England, in every class of manufacture, initiated their own designs in an effort to capture public acceptance. Successful designs were quickly copied by other manufacturers eager to share in the market.

The first English Design Registration Act was passed in 1839, giving designs of all classes of goods three years protection against use by others. Many English manufacturers took advantage of the new law and Dixon was among the first to register designs. Registered numbers 338 and 343 of June, 1840, were for a Dixon powder flask and a coffee pot. The very first ceramic design registered under the more familiar diamond shape registration mark of the Act of 1842 was an earthenware jug mounted with a metal lid by James Dixon & Sons.[11] Most earthenware or porcelain jugs with metal lids were sold by the metal firms who bought the decorated jugs from the potters, mounted them with lids and then offered them for sale as part of their general line of goods.

In 1842, upon the retirement of James Dixon, the firm was assumed by James Willis Dixon, Sr. The mark for goods was changed to read:

JAMES DIXON
& SONS

Fig. 17 One of a pair of Sheffield Plate wine coasters made by James Dixon & Sons in 1844. The coasters are marked on the side with the Dixon Sheffield Plate Mark and the silver button on the bottom is hallmarked for 1844. *Zera L. Hair.*

Fig. 18 James Willis Dixon, the second son of James Dixon born about 1814 and taken into the firm as a partner in 1835 at which time this portrait was probably made. Upon becoming a full partner, James Willis traveled to New York to handle the American affairs for the firm. His son, James Willis Jr. was born in New York in 1838. He returned to Sheffield to assume the head of the firm in 1842 upon the retirement of his father, and remained at the head until his death in 1876.

11. A complete chart of registration numbers will be found in chapter VI.

and remained in use until about 1851. The words BEST BRITANNIA METAL often accompanied the mark during this period. James Dixon died in 1852 and was buried in the family plot at Ecclesfield Parish Church.

By 1849 Dixon had added electroplated wares to its every-growing line of goods. The wares were marked with the Dixon mark and the words ELECTRO PLATE. With the advent of electroplating, nickle silver received greater use, particularly as a base metal for plating. Nickle silver was first introduced in Sheffield in 1826 as German silver and received limited use as a substitute for copper in Sheffield Plate. Dixon was one of the first to manufacture nickle silver spoons and forks in Sheffield. Electroplated goods from about 1855 often included the initials EPBM or EPNS for electroplated Britannia metal or electroplated nickle silver. Spoons and forks made in Sheffield during the period 1830-1875 occasionally will be found to have a BP mark. Until recently the meaning of this mark was unknown to today's collectors but thought to represent best plate or Birmingham plate. Actually the mark refers to *British Plate* which was not a plate at all, but unplated, highly polished nickle silver. James Dixon and others, in an effort to provide attractive and durable spoons and forks that were less expensive than electroplate, produced *British Plate* for that purpose.

Dixon was one of the very last, if not the last major firm to add the word SHEFFIELD to its mark. By 1851, all other major Britannia metal makers in Sheffield had added the city's name along with their own to their products. Not enough information is yet available to pinpoint the exact date of the change in the mark but evidence leads to the year 1851. The change would certainly be no earlier than 1850. James Dixon & Sons entered goods in the great Industrial Exposition of 1851, in London, and received several medals for their products. It may well be that SHEFFIELD was added for that event. In addition to Sheffield being added to the mark, the firm name was stamped in one line so that from about 1851 to 1879 the mark read:

JAMES DIXON & SONS
SHEFFIELD

Fig. 20 A pair of electroplate (over Britannia metal) chambersticks by James Dixon & Sons, c. 1850. The mark is No. 147 plus the word ELECTROPLATE.

Fig. 19 Table forks in British Plate made by JAMES DIXON & SONS of Sheffield. Dixon was one of the first firms to produce British Plate and the Dixon mark on these forks dates 1842-1851. Mark. No. 155.

In 1861 the Dixon firm, as well as many others in England, began to suffer economic set backs directly related to a war torn United States. A restrictive American tariff was placed on imported goods virtually eliminating their main export trade. The southern states were blockaded and the much needed cotton did not reach the mills of northern England. This in turn caused wide spread unemployment and the domestic market was greatly recessed. The Dixon firm pressed hard to increase sales in Australia and the continent as well as other world wide markets.

Adding to their troubles was a catastophe which struck Sheffield at exactly midnight on March 11, 1864. A water reservoir on the outskirts of Sheffield burst, sending a disastrous flood into Sheffield. The unannounced waters struck the town with full force. Two hundred and forty people were killed, most of whom were trapped in their bedrooms. Bridges, houses, factories and whole streets were swept away. The flood, which ended as quickly as it struck, left a path of destruction not even equaled by the enemy bombings of World War II.

The James Dixon & Sons factory located on the River Don, which caught the main stream of the flood, suffered considerable damage to the stamp and die departments located on the lower floors. The houses located nearby, called Waterloo and owned by William Frederick Dixon, received extensive damage and one person was carried away and drowned. A contemporary account records the damage to Dixon's property:

> "The entire front walls were knocked down; the interiors exposed, and the flooring of the bedrooms hung down aslant from its hold on the side which remained uninjured. It was curious, on visiting the scene next morning, to notice bird cages hanging on the walls, with their little inmates trilling their songs as merrily as on any more auspicious morning. Much of the furniture was washed away or destroyed, and the houses themselves were filled with water and mud. The flood came rushing down upon them, and the water rose to the bedrooms. In a few minutes the front wall fell down with a tremendous crash, which startled both those who were asleep and those who were awake, by its loudness and suddeness. Most of the inmates retreated into their back bedrooms, where they were safe from peril of death, although they were flooded and exposed to the cold night wind. An old woman named Mrs. Whittington, 82 years of age, was sleeping in a low room at the home of her daughter. The flood washed away both the old woman and the bed on which she slept. The body of the old woman was found some weeks afterwards, at a distance of many miles from the place where she was drowned."

Fig. 21 These houses, known as Waterloo, show the extensive damage caused when a dam on the outskirts of Sheffield gave way in 1864. The houses located near the Dixon Plant were owned by William Frederick Dixon.

Three members of the Dixon firm, William Frederick Dixon, James Willis Dixon, Sr., and William Fawcett were among the leading men of Sheffield called together the day after flood to seek refief for the victims, and the firm immediately pledged £200 towards a relief fund.

The halt of exported Britannia metal to America in 1861, along with the general decline of the production of Britannia metal in favor of electroplated wares, accounts for the fact that more Dixon wares of the 1804-1860 period are available for the collector than the 1860-1900 period.

The Sheffield Plate trade had given way to electroplate and was almost completely redundant in 1850. The Dixon firm, however, did maintain a limited production of Sheffield Plate for its world wide customers, particularly inns and hotels, even though the market moved more and more to the electroplated goods.

For centuries it had been the practice of all the proud Sheffield metalsmiths to mark their goods with their name or device. Electroplated goods logically and rightfully were marked by the manufacturers. The plated silver was offered as an imitation of sterling and the marks used were usually the maker's initials in separate punches with an occasional additional mark or marks. These were used in the same manner as the official hall marks on silver and at a quick glance very often resembled the official marks.

American born James Willis Dixon, Jr. took over the direction of the company upon the death of his father, James Willis, Sr., in 1876. The Dixon firm had been marking its electroplated goods 🄹🄳🄿&🅂 but two competitors in Sheffield used the same initials. These two firms were Joseph Deakin & Sons and

Fig. 22 Nine hundred employees and staff pose for a picture at the Dixon Plant in 1906.

Fig. 23 The Dixon Plant in 1906

James Deakin & Sons, both of whom had origins in the 18th century. To avoid confusion with competitors and to distinguish Dixon wares from all others, James Dixon & sons registered the "Trumpet and Banner"  mark in 1879. A pair of spoons in the author's possession bear the mark DIXON & SON PATENT as well as the reign mark of William IV and the trumpet and banner device. This would date the spoons about 1830-1834. The registration of the trumpet and banner in 1879 would then seem to be a revival of a much earlier mark which had seen very limited use. Britannia metal goods, as well as electroplated wares from 1879. bear the Dixon trade mark.

In 1889 Lennox Burton Dixon, who was to become the next head of the firm, was taken into partnership. The final years of the 19th century saw the introduction of fringe benefits for employees, including an insurance plan, wages in time of illness, and expense paid convalescent periods at the seaside. Many employees worked a full lifetime at the plant, frequently following in their fathers' footsteps.

Fig. 24 James Willis Dixon, c.1899, was born in New York in 1838, became head of the firm in 1876 and lived the life of a grand English gentlemen. He died in 1917, leaving a considerable estate.

In 1898 and again in 1903, the original premises were enlarged. Production continued at a high level until 1914 when Britain entered the Great War. A large plaque in the Dixon plant honors the many employees who entered military service during that difficult conflict. Full production resumed at the war's end and the firm continues at the present time on the same premises.

James Willis Dixon, Jr. no doubt reaped more personal benefits from the firm than any other director. His tenure covered a period of great prosperity and his position in local politics and social life was such that he narrowly missed knighthood in 1897. Had he sought the mayorship of Sheffield it would have brought him the title. His life was typical of what is thought to be that of the grand old English gentleman.

Born in New York in 1838, James Willis received his education in Sheffield at the Sheffield Collegiate School and in Newweid, Germany. He entered the firm in 1854 and became a partner in 1859. In 1864 he married Fanny Mary Burton, daughter of William S. Burton, a prominent London merchant who acted as an agent for Dixon wares in London. At the same time Dixon served as a captain of the Hallamshire Rifles, adding one hundred employees of the works to the

Fig. 25 **Hillsborough Hall, home of James Willis Dixon, Sr. and James Willis Dixon, Jr.**

battalion.

He was a member of the Founders Company of London and eventually became master of that guild, the first Sheffielder ever to be master of a London guild. He was an avid hunter and athlete. Horticulture also held his interest and his chrysanthemums won many prizes. His father had purchased Hillsborough Hall in 1865 and James Willis continued living there until 1903.

Hillsborough Hall, which is described as being Adam style architecture, was built in 1779 by Thomas Stade. Following the death of his eldest son, Thomas, it was sold, about 1801, to John Rimington who lived there until his death in 1820, and his widow continued to live there until her death in 1838.

The house was then occupied by John Rodgers of Joseph Rodgers & Sons, Ltd., cutlers, and he appears to have named the house Hillsborough Hall, as all earlier references are to Hillsborough House. Rodgers lived there until 1854 when he moved to his new home, Abbeydale House (or Hall).

During the next ten years, Hillsborough Hall was occupied by two additional occupants before being purchased by James Willis Dixon, Sr. in 1865. Dixon made many improvements to the house before his death in 1876. James Willis, Jr. sold his home "Westbourne" in Whitham Road when he inherited his father's estate and moved to Hillsborough. Eventually he sold fifty acres of his estate to the city for use as a public park which opened in 1897. The family retained the house and eleven and one-half acres of land until 1903 when J. W. Dixon sold this to the city.

James Willis Dixon, Jr. died June 29, 1917, and left a personal estate valued at just under £100,000. His son, Lennox Burton Dixon, assumed the head of the firm.

Lennox Burton Dixon died in 1941 and the firm came under the directorship of W. Milo Dixon, a son of Wynyard Dixon, third son of James Willis Dixon, Jr. Mr. W. Milo Dixon continued to actively head the firm until his death at age 75, in January, 1977. He was the last of the surnamed descendants to head the firm.

In the 1920's, a new interest arose in English pewter, both old and new.

52

James Dixon & Sons put renewed emphasis on tea services, tankards, mugs and other items made of Britannia metal which they issued under the trade name *"Cornish Pewter"* for the first time in 1927. The selection "Cornish" as a trade mark had many ramifications. Nearly any association with Cornwall has always brought instant identification with England. Cornwall has also been noted for its tin mines, the main ingredient for pewter. More pointedly, and with less associative implications, is the fact that the firm has been, since 1822, located at Cornish Place, Sheffield. The modern pewter wares made by James Dixon and Sons are distributed under this trade mark. The formula for the metal and the designs of the services are essentially the same as those used in the 19th century.

Fig. 26 **Milo Dixon, 1901-1976, was the last of the direct descendants to head the firm. He served from 1941 until his death in 1976.**

Obviously there were economic set backs and reductions in production during the depression years of the 1920's and 1930's, and when England entered the war in 1939 production turned to the war effort. Luckily the Dixon plant received no damage during the 1940 enemy air raids over Sheffield.

Following the war, production turned once again to domestic wares which slowly found a market in a country determined to make a full recovery. Post-war pewter remained very limited at the Dixon plant as the firm concentrated on silver and electroplated wares. The firm of James Dixon & Sons produced more Britannia metal goods than any other single firm in the 19th century, yet yielded to others in the 20th century production of Sheffield made pewter.

The quality of goods produced by James Dixon & Sons has always been of the highest level both in workmanship and design. A mid-19th century Dixon catalog states that although second class goods were made at the Dixon plant, these goods never received the Dixon mark which was reserved only for first quality goods. Careful examination of antique Dixon wares confirms the Dixon concern for quality.

The search of old city directories and rate books in Sheffield, along with the study of old catalogs, design registrations and other sources have been very valuable in establishing dates for the marks used by the Dixon firm. These sources, along with the notation of data collected from the examination of several hundred old and antique objects, made these dates and guidelines reasonably accurate.

The word SHEFFIELD was not added to Dixon's mark until about 1851. In general then, the absence of SHEFFIELD on Dixon wares would indicate pre-1851 manufacturer. However, post-1851 marks occasionally omit the word Sheffield on small goods and tankards for convenience of available space. The words BEST BRITANNIA METAL were added along with the mark for the period 1835-1851. The trumpet and banner device was used on all goods from 1879 with the exception of the very rare occurence mentioned earlier on page 51. Marks which include Ltd. would be 1921 and later.

Although a few pieces of Dixon ware have been dated, *i.e.*, the date of manufacture or presentation engraved on the article is rare. The numbers on the bottom of goods, even though they may look like dates are merely pattern numbers.

These guides and dates apply to the usual pieces of Britannia metal. There are variations in the marks used on flasks and lidded jugs due to their small size or limited area in which a mark could be placed. All known Dixon marks are illustrated in Chapter VIII.

Fig. 27 Modern *Cornish Pewter* by JAMES DIXON & SONS, LTD. Tankards and small boxes have been continuously produced by The Dixon firm since its founding in 1804.

CHAPTER FOUR
*Methods Of
Construction*

A look at the construction techniques used by Britannia metalsmiths not only commands respect for their expert craftsmanship, but also dispels some of the long perpetuated Britannia metal myths. Prior to the specifics, it should be stated that the often quoted phrase "pewter was cast; Britannia metal spun." is an erroneous generalization which has been given far too much emphasis. Only a portion of the many Britannia metal manufacturing methods involved spinning. Of greater importance is the fact that half of the production years currently being classed as antique occurred before spinning was known to the industry.

The first items made of white metal by James Vickers in Sheffield were cast spoons. This would be reasonable and logical for very little investment was required for spoon making. Several moulds, raw material for melting and a few files and light accessories for finishing the spoons were all that were needed.

Shortly after his initial success with spoons, Vickers discovered that ingots of the metal could also be run through heavy steel rollers producing sheet stock in the same manner as silver and Sheffield Plate. One should keep in mind that, in 1769, the Sheffield Plate trade had been a strong industry for twenty years and silver production was such that an assay office opened there in 1773. The silver trades provided the necessary knowledge, machinery, tools, dies, workman and materials to adapt to white metal.

The manufacturing process began then, as now, with the melting of raw materials—tin, antimony and copper. These were alloyed and cast into small ingots. A different alloy was made for sheet stock than for casting. The formula for ingots which were intended for sheet stock generally consisted of 92% tin, 6% antimony and 2% copper. The antimony gave the alloy hardness and the copper assisted in making the metal workable. The ingots prepared for casting purposes required greater amounts of antimony for increased hardness. The formulas for both casting and sheet stock varied from maker to maker.

Rolling the metal through steel rollers gave the metal the added bonus of being hard and smooth. The art of rolling was highly developed by the Sheffield men and is one aspect of their fine quality metal work which is evident when English wares are compared with a great many American-made pieces.

As new methods were discovered, the earlier techniques continued to be used in addition to, and along with the new developments.

Pieces were carefully cut from sheet stock using a pattern. These were then hand shaped over a mandrel or die stamped. The spouts always were stamped or cast in two parts and soldered together. Teapots and coffee pots of this period had wooden handles and knobs of wood, bone or similar material. Since the teapots had no feet and the handles and knobs were of wood, casting of parts was at a minimum, usually the lid hinge, handle mounts and the peg for the knob. Occasional parts on other wares were also cast, such as the knobs on wine jugs and some parts of the pedestal.

Once the parts were cut out, they were carefully assembled by soldering in the same manner as their counter parts in silver and plate. The same bright cut engraving as used by the silversmiths and platers was also available on items made of Britannia metal. So very few pre-1800 specimens have survived that it is difficult to elaborate on the techniques used. The teapots, jugs, caddies, sugar basins and cream jugs that are available for inspection clearly confirm that the wares were carefully constructed mainly of hand formed pieces.

Soldering Britannia ware was and, still is, a very special skill requiring much practice and expertise. The metal is quite soft with a relatively low melting point. The solder used is of a formula very nearly that of the metal itself. When the wares are made up, the seams show their different color if the solder is of a compostion too far removed from that of the metal. The task is to get the solder to melt and fuse to the metal without the metal itself melting away when the heat is applied. These skilled craftsmen controlled the heat of the flame by using a blowpipe. They regulated the amount of air added to the flame with their own breath.

After articles were soldered together, any rough spots were filed smooth and the seams burnished with a steel tool. This burnishing helped to blend the seam into the metal body making it nearly invisible.

Bright cut engraving involved hand decoration with a wide variety of cutting tools. The patterns were laid out on the metal with transfer paper and the designs then carefully cut into the metal. Hand engraving remained a special feature of Sheffield wares into, and throughout, the 19th century

During this first period, when the Britannia metalsmiths meticulously copied the silver and plated wares, the majority of the journeymen working in the trade received their training in the silver and silver plate trade, for the Britannia metal trade had not yet enjoyed enough growth to supply all the journeymen needed. The goods were made of the same thickness as that used by the platers for Sheffield Plate and not only looked like plated ware, but also were nearly equal in feel and weight. The making of goods prior to 1800 did not require extensive amounts of equipment and this gave the makers an opportunity to prosper and expand without heavy investment into expensive machinery.

The first quarter of the 19th century saw the changes in methods and styles in the Sheffield Plate industry carried over into the Britannia metal trade. Shapes and designs changed with emphasis on a greater variety of styles. Many shapes were decorated by running the sheet stock, before being soldered together, through shaping rollers which produced a horizontal ribbing effect. Feet and edges were added requiring more casting and more soldering and a far greater

Fig. 28 **Hand engraving generally known as** *bright cut.* **From a teapot by** DIXON & SON, c. 1825.

use was made of die stamping to produce the more varied styles, especially the fluted bodies.

Teapots produced during the first quarter of the 19th century were often made up of twenty-five or more separate parts. From two to eight pieces, usually die stamped, sometimes hand formed, were used to construct the main body. Spouts were made in two pieces. Other pieces such as tops, lids and bottoms were hand formed. Knob pegs, handle mounts, bases, pedestals (or feet), hinges and decorative edges were cast in bronze moulds. When lion paw feet were used, each foot was cast in two halves which were then soldered together. Japanned handles and knobs were made of hardwood. Japanning was a special process of baking fine black lacquer on many kinds of wares in the 19th century. Steel pins were usually used to make the handle secure. The grate or strainer which was placed inside the pot at the base of the spout to prevent the tea leaves from escaping is particular example of Sheffield craftsmanship. These grates were made of a separate piece of sheet stock, indiviudally shaped and carefully soldered on the inside of the teapot.

59

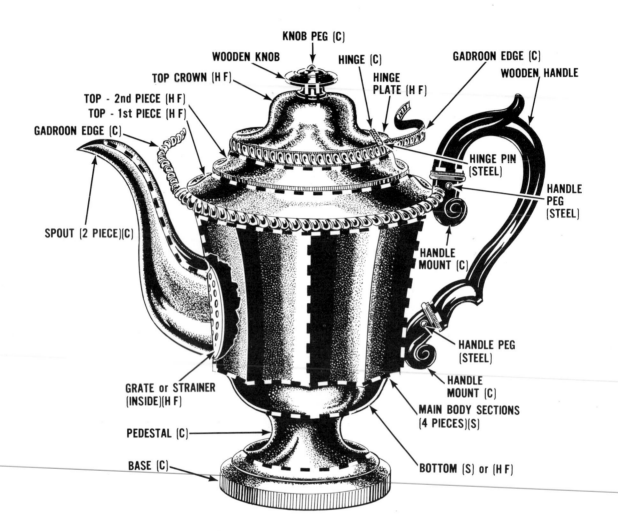

KNOB PEG (C)

WOODEN KNOB

HINGE (C)

GADROON EDGE (C)

WOODEN HANDLE

TOP CROWN (H F)

HINGE PLATE (H F)

TOP - 2nd PIECE (H F)

TOP - 1st PIECE (H F)

GADROON EDGE (C)

HINGE PIN (STEEL)

HANDLE PEG (STEEL)

SPOUT (2 PIECE)(C)

HANDLE MOUNT (C)

GRATE or STRAINER (INSIDE)(H F)

HANDLE PEG (STEEL)

HANDLE MOUNT (C)

PEDESTAL (C)

MAIN BODY SECTIONS (4 PIECES)(S)

BASE (C)

BOTTOM (S) or (H F)

Fig. 29 A teapot by DIXON & SMITH, c. 1815, constructed of twenty-five separately hand crafted parts. The entire process required skills in hand forming, casting, die stamping, soldering, wood work, Japanning, burnishing, cleaning, polishing and (not shown here) engraving. Even though new methods, including spinning, were later developed, the techniques and methods of this period continued in use throughout the 19th century.

C-CAST   S-STAMPED   H F- HAND FORMED

In spite of the fact that by 1825 Britannia metal manufacturing had become a big industry, one can see that the product depended on skilled craftsmen to make and assemble all the necessary parts.

The gadroon edges so popular during this period were made in separate strips and carefully soldered to the main bodies of articles, for the metal smiths continued to copy the platers both in style and method. One notable exception to the added edges were candlesticks where the gadroons were almost always cast into the design. Wages were at this time still very low and, even with the inclusion of hand engraving, a teapot of the above construction brought the wholesale price of twelve shilliings. The cost of engraving a teapot increased the cost of the decorated teapots about one shilling.

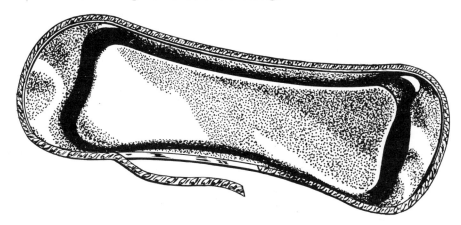

Fig. 30 Gadroon, thread and other decorative edges were neatly cast and carefully soldered to the wares. This not only completed the Sheffield Plate look, but also made the goods much stronger.

The period 1825-1900 brought three changes: a further increase in the use of casting, the introduction of spinning,and designs and styles which were not dependent on the silver trade but were peculiar to the Britannia metal industry.

Phillip Ashberry began working as a spoon maker in 1829 and built a large business on his early reputation as a maker of good quality spoons. Ashberry's production included spoons and ladles of every description. They were accepted as high quality because of their hardness. His formula contained a high proportion of antimony and became known in the trade as Ashberry metal. Dr. Hedges gives the formula for Ashberry metal as containing up to twenty-five percent antimony.

In almost all instances the metal used for casting contained an increased amount of antimony. The extra antimony shows up on the patina of antique Britannia metal where the cast parts have a slight orange peel effect which does not appear on the sections made of rolled stock.

By 1835 Britannia metal was widely recognized for its own merits and no longer needed to stand in the shadow of Sheffield Plate. As the need to produce exact copies lessened, the Britannia metal men learned that the earlier light weight copies were subject to wear and dents. The public, growing in affluence, demanded "better quality" from their Britannia metal. Correspondingly manufacturers increased the thickness of the metal in many styles and several

61

Fig. 31 **The horizontal seam and the orange peel patina can be seen in this coffee pot made entirely of cast pieces by BROADHEAD & ATKIN, c. 1840.**

leading makers, including James Dixon & Sons and Broadhead & Atkin, made tea and coffee wares constructed entirely of pieces cast in moulds, something the traditional pewterers had unsuccessfully attempted.

In the mid-1820's spinning was introduced in the metal industries of Sheffield and the Britannia trade quickly added the new technique to their manufacturing needs. The art of spinning had been known in various forms since ancient times. A circular, flat piece of metal was attached to a wooden chuck of a specific shape. The chuck was then placed on a high speed lathe. As the chuck spun, the workman pressed the metal against the chuck with a special rod like tool which shaped the metal against the chuck. For simple designs this process took only a few seconds. The process was, and still is, much cheaper and faster than stamping with dies. In general spinning was limited to round objects and, therefore, could only be used for those parts or bodies which were round. Nevertheless, it added a new technique which provided increased production. It allowed for the production of inexpensive goods made of fewer component parts. Fewer parts meant less soldering and quicker construction.

Simple, round teapots required half the parts of the more elaborate teapots. Style did not allow for all teapots to be round, however, because about 1835 the octagon and other George II styles were revived from the popular silver designs of one hundred years earlier.

The new technique of spinning did not revolutionize the trade in the 19th century, but gave expansion to the metalsmith's craft which continued to employ all of the techniques of earlier years.

In 1844 James Shaw of Shaw & Fisher received a patent for an interesting invention which worked but was not widely used except in his own factory. His patent was number 10,235, dated 24 December, 1844, and concerned the manufacture of hot water dishes and dish covers. Dish covers were generally available in six sizes from ten to twenty-four inches. Each size and each pattern required a pair of steel dies the size and shape of the cover. Covers were stamped out by very large drop stamping machines. It was a very costly process, for dish covers were oval shaped and could not be spun. Shaw invented a method by which oval shapes could be spun, allowing a more practical process for dish covers.

Shaw's patent further explained his process for installing a wire in the edge of dishes and covers for strength and to help them to retain their shape. The patent also covered his process of boiling Britannia metal wares in whale oil after being made up. Boiling in oil at high temperature just below the melting point, was said to harden the metal.

Thomas Skinner of Shefffield received patent number 13,718 on 14 August, 1851, for a process by which ornamental designs could be etched onto Britannia metal. Skinner used transfer designs from engraved plates which were placed on goods already made up. By a special process the design was etched out by the controlled use of acid.

Metal handles were first used on Britannia metal teapots and coffee pots in 1840, although wood handles continued to receive limited use long after that date. Samuel Russell, by patent number 2531, of 28 October, 1856, devises a method of ornamenting horn handles with mother of pearl, ivory, silver and "other materials".

Both Skinner's and Russell's inventions received later patents for improvements. Various other inventions related to the Britannia metal industry also received patent protection.

Although the production of Britannia metal goods went into decline about 1870, the goods that were made continued to be made in the same manner as they had always been. Round shapes and parts were spun or stamped, non-round shapes were die stamped and feet, legs, knobs, handles, spouts and other parts were cast. All parts were carefully soldered together and hand finished. Engraving, when used on Britannia metal goods, continued to be done by hand.

A process was used from about 1850 which gave the surface of tankards and flasks an over all pattern of light wavy lines. The process was known as engine turning but did not attempt to duplicate or imitate hand engraving as did machine engraving. Machine engraving allowed a design to be pressed into sheet stock which was passed through reversely engraved rollers. This process which did imitate hand engraving was used primarily on cheap electroplated goods, much of which was plated on Britannia metal. These cheap goods with the silver worn away contributed greatly to the low esteem given to Britannia metal in some circles.

In the 1920's, a revived interest in new pewter brought new life to the Sheffield Britannia industry. Hand hammering is the characteristic feature of the pewter produced from the 1920's until the beginning of World War II.

The hammering of metals is an ancient art and was originally done to strengthen the metal. The hammering of pewter wares from the 16th century was so common that the pewterers were known as hammermen, but by the end of the 18th century very little pewter was hammered. The concept was revived as a decorative accent during the wane of the art nouveau period. Copper, brass and silver items often were hand hammered in the early years of the 20th century.

Pewter wares to be hammered were partially or completely assembled and filled with hot liquid material similar to pitch which had been used in the earlier centuries in connection with hand chased silver wares. The material quickly hardened and the items were then hammered all over. Upon completion of hammering the hard material was melted and poured out, the pewter ware then being cleaned and sent to the finishing room for a final polishing.

Although hand hammering receives limited use in modern pewter, a wide range of decorative and functional pewter wares are still made in the traditional way in Sheffield. The vast percentage of goods are no longer tea wares but tankards and mugs which are entirely spun except for the handles.

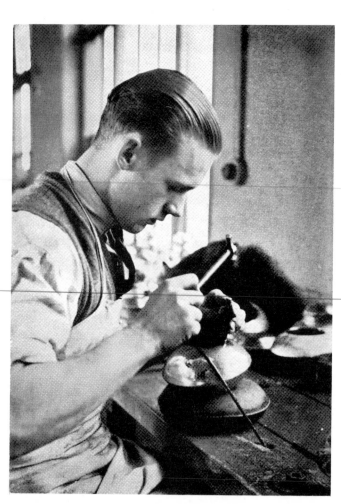

Fig. 32 A Sheffield craftsman hand hammering wares in the 1920's.

CHAPTER FIVE
Characteristic
Features

The greater portion of 18th and 19th century Britannia metal ware made in Sheffield is realtively easy to identify, for nearly all manufacturers marked their goods with their name. A few exceptions do exist, notably candlesticks which were seldom marked. In some instances only a single piece of a tea service received a mark. When the set became separated over the years, the unmarked pieces remained unidentified. As the makers often changed marks, the period of manufacture can be ascertained by specific marks. Where the marks did not change over a long period of time or in the instance of unmarked goods, reference has to be made to stylistic characteristics such as basic shape, feet, knob, handle, spout and decoration, if any.

The feet, bases, knobs, handles, spouts and engraving which may have been added to basic forms or shapes can often provide clues to the period in which goods were made. During their many years of use, wares were often subject to repairs and replacements. A teapot made in 1825 which lost its knob in 1855 would most likely have an 1855 knob put on as a replacement. This is just as true with feet, bases, handles and spouts, and this possibility must be kept in mind when typing to establish a date.

The majority of guidelines given here refer rather specifically to teapots and in a general way to other wares.

BASIC STYLE

The influence of style is reflected most strongly in the teapots and tea services, although nearly all of the other wares were also dictated by the style of the period.

From the introduction of white metal in Sheffield, to about 1800, the makers produced goods under the stylistic influence of the

Fig. 33 **Teapot by DIXON & SON, c. 1825, with a metal handle! Close inspection shows that not only is the handle a replacement, but that the handle is not English, but American.** *Alan W. Anderson.*

architectural designer, Robert Adam (1728-1792). The designs of the Adam period were graceful and employed clean, classical lines.

Adam began his career as an architect in 1759. His brother James (1730-1794) joined him in 1761, and in 1773 they published their first volume of *The Works of Robert and James Adam*. Much of their philosophy of decoration, which dominated English designs for half a century, is contained in these *Works*. The Adam brothers believed that every detail of a house and it's furnishings should come from one mind.

Adam accessories were always adjuncts to architectural designs. In their books, Robert and James express their concept of the unity of architecture, furniture, and accessories. When they designed a building, they designed all that went into it. This unity was new to English architecture and came from France where the approach was used in palaces.

The distinguishing features of Adam style are a preference for straight lines and square silhouettes. Adam used swags, festoons and continuous spiral or wavy ornaments. All these decorations are free in form. Mythological figures such as rams' heads, lions' heads and claws, centaurs, and griffins mingle with plant forms and Greek and Roman vases. Bright cut engraving was used extensively on metal work, often featuring the festoon and swag motifs.

Large numbers of metalware accessories were produced in the Adam style by the various metalsmiths. Fireplace fenders and candlesticks in brass were particularly influenced by Adam. Silver and Sheffield Plate candlesticks and tea services were almost exclusively Adam in concept during the period 1775-1800.

During the period 1800-1825 Adam style gave way to late Georgian canoe (cottage or boat) shapes. Bright cut engraving continued in use but without the drape effect. Feet were added to teapots, and small tea sets, which were not common in the 18th century, now included matching teapot, creamer and sugar. By 1810 fluted and reverse fluted designs had appeared in addition to the boat shapes, and gadroon edges were very popular. The Dixon & Smith catalog of 1817 shows the majority of teapots to be variations on the boat shape along with two other minor styles, a bulbous or pear shape with fluting on the lower half and a cannister shape with lower broad fluting. These non-boat shapes often sat on a pedestal base which became very popular twenty years later. After 1830, gadroon edges found little favor and soon disappeared from use.

A particular shape that appeared about 1815 and remained popular throughout all the years of the industry was the simple globular shape on a rim base. From 1825 to 1840 the previous boat shapes and fluted designs lost favor to new and original patterns along with copies of silver designs of the early 18th century.

About 1825, when the technique of metal spinning came into use, Sheffield Plate designs were less frequently copied. From 1830 to 1845 emphasis was placed on coffee pots and large, complete tea and coffee services, primarily for the American market. The earlier fluted bulbous shapes evolved into graceful and paneled designs on pedestal bases. The pedestal became the most prominent base, as ball, lion paw and shell feet fell into complete use. Of particular importance was the use of the eight sided style, again as a revival of the early 18th century silver styles.

68

Many factors brought about great changes in style during the years 1840-1855. Most of the Britannia metal firms were well established and could afford to experiment with the many styles the public seemed to demand. The Victorian feeling for highly decorative wares featuring flora and fauna was in vogue and the introduction of electroplating gave emphasis to highly decorated wares. James Dixon & Sons registered a melon teapot in 1848, and another teapot in 1850 which greatly resembled an egg plant.

In addition to new designs based on fruits, flowers and animals, makers were able to offer prospective buyers a complete line of domestic wares which ranged from coffin tags to large sets of great hot water dishes with matching covers.

The Shaw & Fisher catalog of 1848 shows 105 different teapots with the option of seven different handles and fifty knobs, each pot being available in eight different sizes. By 1855, nearly every type of useful household ware which would have been practical to have been made in metal was available. There are two exceptions. Nowhere has there been any examples or references to Britannia metal bedpans or chamberpots, both of which had always been available in earthenware, traditional pewter, and other metals, including silver.

While the 1840-1855 period placed emphasis on highly ornate styles dependent on decorative handles, feet, knobs and special botanical shapes, engraving fell to limited use and little is seen on wares of this period other than on dram flasks.

As popular as the ornate styles may have been during their relatively short years of production, fewer of these have survived than goods of the earlier years. The reasons for this are: (1) They did not have the clean lines of the earlier styles, hence lacked the feeling of being traditional, and soon became dated, (2) The earlier wares of classic lines never went completely out of use, (3) When used, the ornate wares were difficult to clean and polish and once worn and dirty, lost a great amount of appeal.

During the period of 1870-1914 the production of Britannia metal gave way to electroplated wares whose makers continued the production of ornate wares. The Britannia metal that was produced, reverted to simple lines and styles, such as the pear shape which was popular from about 1850 to 1880 and the Adam revival which was popular from 1860 to 1900. Engraving returned to favor and is frequently seen on goods from 1860 into the 20th century.

The most distinctive style to emerge in the latter half of the 19th century was the Adam revival teapot. The revival appeared about 1860, reached its peak about 1880 and continued in popularity into the 20th century. The teapots were made much like the teapots of one hundred years earlier with two obvious exceptions. The spouts were curved, even if only slightly, and the handles were metal. Far more of these teapots were produced in electroplated Britannia metal than non-plated metal.

The art nouveau styles of 1890-1910 included creations in pewter but it would seem that very few, if any, were made in Sheffield, the principal centers being Birmingham and London.

Fig. 34 Adam style, c. 1770-1800.

Fig. 35 Boat or canoe shape, c. 1810-1830.

Fig. 36 The simple globular shape with rim base was introduced about 1815 and remained popular into the 20th century.

Fig. 37 Eight sided pedestal, c. 1830-1845.

Fig. 38 Pear, c. 1850-1880.

Fig. 39 Adam revival, c. 1870-1910.

70

FEET AND BASES

During the period 1769-1800, teapots had not feet or base but were flat bottomed, sitting on a small tray or directly on the table. Other wares were made in a similar style.

It was about 1800 that footed teapots appeared. The three basic types of feet used were: lion paw, shell pattern, and ball. At this period, with frequent hard times brought about by an almost continous war effort, the move to feet may have been one of economy, for it eliminated the need for the teapot stand. The three styles of feet remained popular until about 1830. Simple rim bases for teapots and tea wares, i.e., creamer, sugar and waste bowl, appeared about 1815 and remained in constant popularity. About the same time, pedestal bases appeared and reached their peak of popularity during the 1830-1840 decade. After 1840 very ornate bases and feet, heavily cast, came into fashion. About 1855, upon the return to simpler lines, the wares also took on less ornate feet and bases, the simple rim base being widely used. Upon the introduction of Adam revival teapots, feet once again went out of style with the teapot sitting directly on the table or stand. Matching coffee pots occasionally had pedestal bases.

For the majority of wares produced in the 20th century the simple rim bases predominate, although various feet of simple design are occasionally found.

Fig. 40 c. 1800-1830.

Fig. 41 c. 1810-1830.

Fig. 42 c. 1810-1835.

Prior to 1800, teapots sat directly on the table or on a small matching stand. At the turn of the century, styles changed, allowing the use of feet. There were very few exceptions to the ball, shell and lion paw feet which were in use from c. 1800 to c. 1835.

71

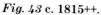

Fig. 43 c. 1815++.

Fig. 44 c. 1830-1845.

The plain rim base (43) was introduced in the Britannia metal trade about 1815, and never went out of use. The pedestal (44) enjoyed great popularity during the years c. 1830-c. 1845, being particularly popular in America. Feet began to appear in the form of ornate and heavy castings about 1840 (45).

Fig. 45 c. 1840-1845.

Fig. 46 c. 1850.

A special petal design (46) was registered by James Dixon & Sons in 1850. Lighter cast feet (47) were used during the period 1850-1865. The Adam revival (48) again placed the teapot directly on the table or trivet.

Fig. 47 c. 1850-1865.

Fig. 48 c. 1870-1910.

72

KNOBS

The Adam period knobs were made in simple round or oval shapes entirely of wood, ivory or bone. The knobs were unpretentious as were their counterparts in Sheffield Plate and silver. On tea caddies, the knobs were occasionally made of ivory, stained green, in the form of a pineapple, the symbol of hospitality. Metal urn shaped knobs were used on claret jugs.

When the canoe or boat shapes began to appear about 1800, the knobs were almost always made of Japanned wood and were plain and oblong in shape to conform with the boat shape. As round shaped tea and coffee pots appeared, starting about 1815, the knobs used on the non-boat shapes were simple and round with an incised groove centered on the outer edge. From about 1828-1845, the wooden knobs, always black, changed to a flower shape somewhat reminiscent of the zinnia. There were very few deviations from the three basic wooden knobs used from 1800-1845.

No metal knobs were used on teapots or coffee pots prior to 1830, therefore any Britannia metal teapot or coffee pot of English manufacture with an original metal knob cannot be dated earlier than that date. In 1830 James Dixon & Son, who had added Sheffield Plate to manufactured wares, began to use filled silver knobs on some of their Britannia metal teapots and coffee pots. This practice was soon taken up by other manufacturers engaged in the production of both Britannia metal and Sheffield Plate.

These silver plated knobs were exactly the same as those used on Sheffield Plate and were made by carefully stamping a thin sheet of silver into a steel die. The stamped out silver shape was then filled with lead. This gave a solid knob with a silver exterior and a lead interior, hence, the description known in the industry as *filled silver*, meaning silver, filled with lead. This technique was widely used in the Sheffield Plate trade for a great variety of decorative mountings. Broadhead and Atkin called their knobs *silver filbert* and this term may be seen stamped on the bottom on some of their pots of the 1840 period. Other makers also used the term.

Filled silver knobs continued in use (along with wooden knobs) until about 1850 when electroplated Britannia knobs and knobs of unplated Britannia metal took their place.

The first filled silver knobs, as well as all wooden knobs (which had metal pegs), were soldered directly to the lids. The screw type knob which had been in use on wares of silver and Sheffield Plate did not come into general use on Britannia metal wares until the introduction of Britannia metal knobs in 1840. Teapots or coffee pots with original screw type metal knobs cannot be dated earlier than 1840. Caution must be used here, for the knob was the most frequently damaged and replaced part of the teapot and pre-1840 teapots may show up with later replacement screw type knobs.

In the 1840's, knobs of Britannia metal became popular and these were available either as screw type or fixed to the teapot lid. A wide range of knobs became available, complimenting the movement to a great range of ornate designs. The Shaw and Fisher catalog of 1848 lists, (in addition to wood) knobs of pearl, ivory, and forty-four different knobs in plated silver. Of these, eleven were

Fig. 49 Typical knobs used from c. 1785 to c. 1860.

A.

Bone c. 1785.

B.

Wood c. 1800-1830.

C.

Wood c. 1810-c. 1830.

D.

Wood c. 1828-1845.

E.

Filled silver c. 1830.

F.

Filled silver *silver filbert* c. 1840.

G.

Filled silver c. 1840.

H.

Metal c. 1838-1845.

I.

Metal c. 1845-1850.

J.

Whippet c. 1840-1850.

K.

Whippet c. 1860.

L.

Exotic bird c. 1860.

74

Fig. 50 Selection of knobs from the Shaw & Fisher catalog of 1848 and four late 19th century knobs.

M.

Persian.

N.

New Vine.

O.

Poppy.

P.

Columbine.

Q.

Buttercup.

R.

Reclus.

S.

Convolvolus.

T.

Lilly bud.

U.

Bone c. 1870-1900.

V.

Carved bone c. 1870-1900.

W.

Metal c. 1880-1900.

X.

Metal c. 1900-1910.

75

METAL KNOBS AVAILABLE 1848
(SHAW & FISHER)

Fast knobs (soldered to the lid)

Convolvolus	Nutmeg
Thistle	Strawberry
Squirrel	Melon
Grape	Rose and Leaf

Loose knobs (screw type)

Vine	Apple
Reclus	Fruit Basket
Strawberry	Panzy
Crown and Cushion	Fuschia
Crown only	Bell knob
Acorn	Thistle
Lilly	New Acorn
Horn of Plenty	New Vine
Basket and Fruit	Butler Cup
Rose Tree	Lilly Bud
Peacock	Poppy
Persian	Pink
Flower Pot	Gentiane
Bird of Paradise	Columbine
Orange	Vegetable Marrow
Plumb	New Apple
New Lilly	Spreading Vine

Black knobs (wood) were also available.

offered as being fixed to the lids and thirty-three were loose or screw type. Shaw & Fisher were noted Sheffield Plate and electroplate (at a later period) manufacturers and their wares of this period are frequently seen with filled silver knobs. In some instances, the silver is worn completely away, showing only the lead.

The other makers in the city no doubt offered the same or similar knobs in silver or Britannia metal. These ornate knobs enjoyed continued success throughout the Victorian Period and some are still in use on present day electroplated goods.

With the Adam Revival teapot of the 1860-1900 period, a simple oval knob of metal, ivory, bone, wood or pearl was used. These were always the screw type. The pedestals were always made separately and of metal, whereas the true Adam knobs were made in one piece, entirely of bone or ivory, of course the peg was metal and was soldered to the lid. It should also be noted that during the second half of the 19th century earthenware and glass knobs were used on occasion.

HANDLES

It remains an unresolved inquiry as to why metal handles did not appear on English made Britannia metal teapots and coffee pots prior to 1840. Bradbury states that early 19th century Sheffield Plate tea services included metal handles when made up as a set, but wooden handles were used when teapots and coffee pots were made singly. Certainly numerous examples of antique silver and Sheffield Plate with metal handles are known while the handles on Britannia metal teapots remained wooden until the introduction of the *anti caloric* metal handles by Broadhead & Atkin in 1840. The entire industry immediately adopted the concept of metal handles.

The first (1840-1842) metal handles were copies of the wooden handles then in use but soon became very ornate (1842-1850), and then reverted to more simple and functional designs (1850). A special note should be made that metal handles on 19th century English teapots and coffee pots were never painted black as they were in America.

Mention should be given to the unique handles patented by Samuel Russell in 1856 and 1859. The 1856 patent covers the making of handles out of horn which was then "studded with ornaments of mother of pearl, ivory, silver or other material which may be pressed into it in the form of leaves or other approved design." The patent also specified a particular method of attaching the handles which limited the transmission of heat into the handle.

The 1859 patent refers to the making of handles from scrap ivory, cane, bone, etc., which was turned into rings mounted over a basic handle form and glued together.

No surviving examples of these patented handles are known. However, the concept included in the first patent, of attaching these handles to the pots, was used by many makers (with Russell's permission) and PATENT NON-CONDUCTING HANDLE may be seen on the wares of many different Sheffield makers during the period 1856-1866. The marks may appear on the handle or on the bottom of the pot.

Fig. 51 Handles in use from 1769-1855.

A.   B.   C.   D.

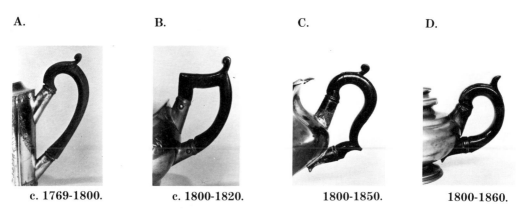

c. 1769-1800.   c. 1800-1820.   1800-1850.   1800-1860.

A. Graceful long curve of the 18th century Adam style. B., C., D. Wooden handles used exclusively until 1840 and continued in use as a matter of economy after metal handles were introduced in 1840, never falling completely out of use.

E.   F.   G.   H.

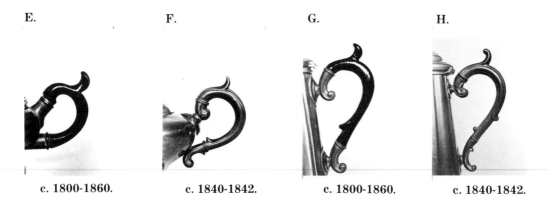

c. 1800-1860.   c. 1840-1842.   c. 1800-1860.   c. 1840-1842.

F. and H. show the first metal handles which were made as copies of the wooden handles (E. and G.) previously in use. Metal handles on 19th century English goods were never painted black as they were on American wares.

I.   J.   K.   L.

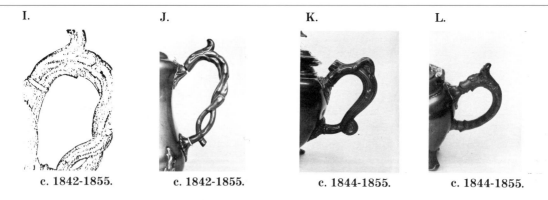

c. 1842-1855.   c. 1842-1855.   c. 1844-1855.   c. 1844-1855.

I., J. One of the first anti caloric (heat resistant) handles introduced by Broadhead & Atkin in 1840. By 1842 the plain metal handles lost favor to the more ornate, with the vine (K) and the dragon (L) being very popular.

Fig. 52 Handles in use from 1844-1910.

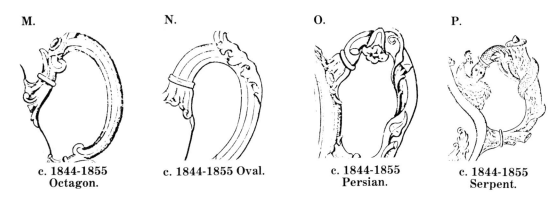

M.

N.

O.

P.

c. 1844-1855
Octagon.

c. 1844-1855 Oval.

c. 1844-1855
Persian.

c. 1844-1855
Serpent.

M., N., O., P. These examples are taken from the Shaw & Fisher catalog of 1848 and show the fashion for ornate designs featuring flora and fauna. The octagon and oval were particularly popular.

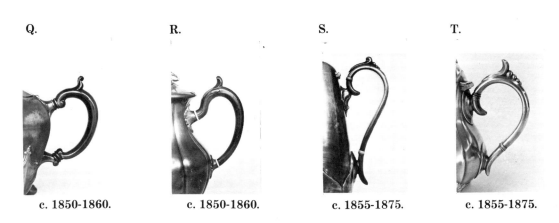

Q.

R.

S.

T.

c. 1850-1860.

c. 1850-1860.

c. 1855-1875.

c. 1855-1875.

Q., R., S., T. From 1850 when electroplated wares largely superseded the popularity of Britannia metal goods, Britannia metal wares reverted to clean simple lines, even though the silver plated goods continued to be made in very orante styles.

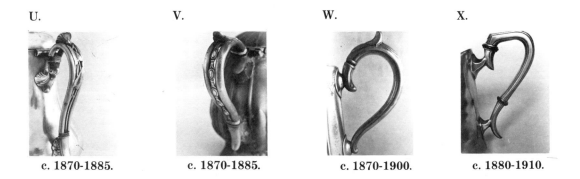

U.

V.

W.

X.

c. 1870-1885.

c. 1870-1885.

c. 1870-1900.

c. 1880-1910.

U., V. James Dixon & Sons introduced the handles of open design about 1870 and they were used until about 1885. W., X. One distinguishing difference between the Adam revival teapots of 1870-1900 and the 18th century originals was the use of metal handles on the Adam revival.

Wooden handles and knobs continued to be offered after 1840 but customers were enticed to purchase the stylish metal handles and knobs (at an increase in price). Using a clever business practice, prices in the Shaw & Fisher catalog of 1848 are for all teapots with black (wooden) handles and knobs. The prices for silver knobs and metal handles listed as being *extra*. Nearly all the engraved illustrations, however, show the teapots with the fancy knobs and handles.

SPOUTS

A few comments should be added about spouts, for they are characteristic of certain periods. The spouts on English teapots and coffee pots were with very few exceptions always made in two halves which were either stamped or cast and then soldered together. This gave the inside of the spouts a very smooth surface which allowed free flow of the contents and also helped to keep the inside of the spout clean.

The pre-1800 spouts were straight and came up from the bottom of the pot in typical Adam fashin. With the introduction of the boat shapes after 1800 the more familiar curved goose neck spouts came into use. These were smooth sided, the top side of the spout being flat or nearly flat. These spouts continued in general use until about 1830 but should not be confused with the round spouts with smooth sides of the later part of the century.

About 1825 spouts with a fluted lower half, copied from early 18th century silver styles, came into use and lasted until 1845. From about 1840, with the introduction of metal handles and the general movement to more ornate styles, spouts took on a wide variety of designs with no singular pattern emerging as being characteristic.

With the Adam revival, one factor which quickly distinguishes the revival from those of a century earlier is the spout. Adam revival spouts were always curved, even if only slightly at the tip, whereas true Adam style normally incorporated perfectly straight spouts, even to the end.

In trying to assess and date Sheffield made articles an important point should be kept in mind. *The maker's mark never lies.* All makers were willing to make up custom orders, particularly as replacements or as additions to a set or service that had been made many years earlier. When replacements or fill-in articles were made they were marked with the maker's current mark. Also, some styles remained in production for many years. Hence, we may have something with a manufacturing date which is quite different from the characteristics of the article. Those who appreciate fine English porcelain and earthenware have found this to be also true with tea services and dinner services made in Staffordshire.

Finally, a few comments on electroplated wares. Many wares were made as silver plate (EP) with Britannia metal as the base metal, and teapots and other items are now found with the silver completely worn away, even from the inside and hard to reach places. When in this state of wear they often cannot be distinguished from those made at the same time as unplated Britannia metal. Those stamped EPBM were obviously silver plated. Other clues are not so

Fig. 53 Spouts 1769-1845.

A.

A. Typical 18th century Adam style spout, perfectly straight.

c. 1769-1800.

B.

c. 1800-1830.

C.

B., C. Smooth spouts were used exclusively from c. 1800 to about c. 1820. They continued to be used a few years beyond 1820 when the fluted base spouts (D. and E.) became popular. The spouts illustrated in D. and E. were copied from mid 18th century silver designs. F. A heavily cast, ornate variation of E.

c. 1800-1830.

D.

c. 1820-1845.

E.

c. 1820-1845.

F.

c. 1840.

81

Fig. 54 Spouts 1850-1900.

G.   H.   I.

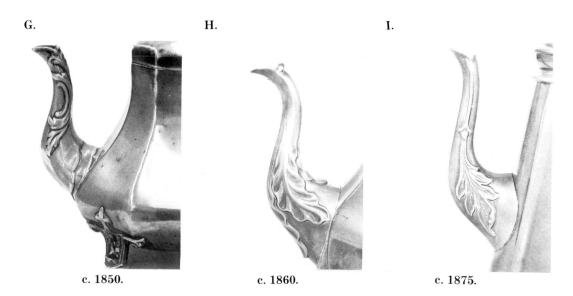

c. 1850.   c. 1860.   c. 1875.

G., H., I. Embossed spouts of many designs were used from c. 1845-c. 1875. Leaves were frequently featured.

J.   K.   L.

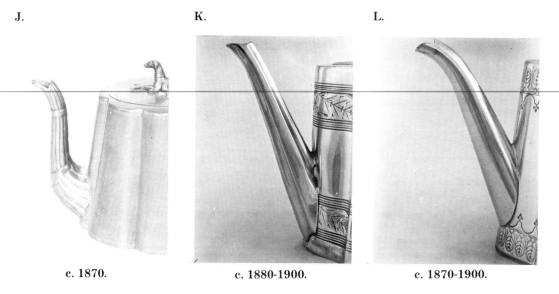

c. 1870.   c. 1880-1900.   c. 1870-1900.

J., K., L. Adam revival spouts had many variations but almost always had some curve to the spout, even if only at the lip as in illustration K.

obvious. Close inspection of the knob, feet and handle will often reveal that in plated wares these parts were made of lead instead of Britannia metal. The lead cast well, was cheaper than Britannia metal and when plated could not be detected. With all the silver gone the lead can be distinguished by its dull grey color and it's softness.

Even though electroplating was not developed for manufacturing until 1843, Britannia metal wares pre-dating electroplate are sometimes found to be silver plated. Walker & Co. of Sheffield, made no goods of their own but provided a plating service for others. Their advertisement of 1845 strongly suggests that wares in daily use could be brought into the platers to be silver plated, for Britannia metal plated very well, eventually becoming the base metal along with nickle silver for the vast electroplate trade. It would seem that a reference to goods being replated in the ad referred to worn Sheffield Plate.

It is very likely that a substantial amount of pre-1843 wares were subsequently plated in the 19th century when great amounts of antique Britannia metal and Sheffield Plate have been gathered up along with worn electro plate and sent to the platers to be "replated", unfortunately in some instance, receiving a cheap job. Traditionalists can but regret the indiscriminate replating done by a few dealers who offer "attractive Victorian silver plate to the trade". One shop in recent years, in Sheffield, specialized in newly plated old wares and often was loaded with replated Sheffield Plate and Britannia metal in addition to EPNS and EPBM. One consoling grace for the purist collector of Britannia metal (and there are some of us), it can easily be unplated.

CHAPTER SIX
MARKS

English antiques rank among the most desirable in the world for good reason. The quality of workmanship has always been very high. The designs are tasteful and they are easy to identify and authenticate. No one but the English would be so careful as to mark their goods, register their designs, devise date letters, pass regulating ordinances and, in general, leave such a wealth of sources for dating and identifying wares.

The Sheffield craftsmen were typical of all of the above. With design and workmanship being thoroughly discussed in Chapters IV and V, this chapter will relate to the marking of goods made in Sheffield.

When writing about antiques, we speak about the usual and that which is typical, but one must always be prepared for the exceptions and this is true of the marks used by the hundreds of makers who worked in Sheffield. It is for the unknown exception one must be watchful.

In looking at the marks stamped on the bottom of Britannia ware many things can be determined at a quick glance. Generally, the more information included in the mark on teapots, the more recent the article. The main exception being the Broadhead & Atkin mark of 1834-1843 which often includes four or five lines.

The typical mid 19th century mark includes the following information: maker's name, the word SHEFFIELD, a capacity number which refers to half-pints, a workman's number or mark, and a pattern number. The location or position of the numbers varies greatly and has no significance.

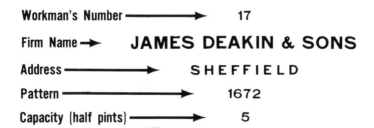

The 18th and early 19th century makers used only their name when marking their wares. In many instances only the surname was used. Occasionally a workman's number or mark accompanied the maker's name. In some cases the marks were intaglio (the letters standing out in relief) but most examples were incised (the letters stamped into the metal). Throughout the 18th, 19th and the first half of the 20th century, the ampersand (&) was used without exception as well as the constant use of upper case letters.

By the second quarter of the 19th century incised marks were used almost exclusively with the exception of intaglio marks on spoons and ladles and the limited use of intaglio marks on some spirit flasks and special items. The 20th century also saw the occasional use of intaglio marks.

Fig. 55 Incised

Fig. 56 Intaglio

Fig. 57 This rare SHAW & FISHER mark, c. 1844-c. 1854. was cast as an excutcheon and soldered to the under side of large hot water dishes. The same mark, stamped in tin, may also be found inside large dish covers.

Marks cast in an escutcheon and soldered to wares were used in some instances as well as a few marks incised on a pad and soldered to wares. These marks are very unusual.

Most Sheffield manufacturing firms began under the direct ownership of one person or partnership and the name of the firm took the name of the founder or founders. As the firm grew and sons or outside partners were taken in, the name and the mark was altered to reflect the change. These periodic changes in name and marks have become a very important factor in attributing marked wares to specific time periods.

Pattern numbers were the first additional marks, other than a workman's mark, to be included with the maker's name. The first regular use of pattern numbers appeared on goods made by Dixon & Son in 1828 and 1829, although limited use of pattern numbers prior to this date do exist. For some reason pattern numbers were not included on all goods. Dixon had begun a healthy export trade, particularly to America, and it is very likely that pattern numbers were included on the exported goods to avoid any confusion and resulting delays for orders. It soon became the practice of makers to put pattern numbers on nearly all goods, and after 1830, most firms included the numbers on their wares.

Each firm had its own system for assigning pattern numbers. Shaw & Fisher seem to have allowed their numbers to fall in logical numerical sequence. James Dixon & Sons' pattern numbers do not always fall into chronological sequence and their system has not yet been deciphered. R. Broadhead & Co. ran into a problem of not being able to designate the type of knob that was issued with each teapot, for there was a great range of knobs available. From about 1855

Broadhead solved this by adding extra numbers representing the type of knob to the existing pattern number.

Pattern numbers of three, four or five digits, found on the bottom of wares, are just that, pattern numbers, and all temptations to make them dates must be resisted.

The addition of the word SHEFFIELD to the maker's mark was introduced by Joseph Wolstenholme sometime between the years 1825 and 1830. In 1834 Broadhead & Atkin included not only the firm's name and workman's mark, but also their address, the word SHEFFIELD, the capacity of teapots and coffee pots, and from 1840 and 1841, the words *Silver Filbert Knob* or *Anti Caloric Handle*. The inclusion of so much information in the mark is peculiar to Broadhead & Atkin. By 1840 nearly all Sheffield's makers included the city name on their goods. One exception was James Dixon and Sons who did not add SHEFFIELD to their mark until about 1851.

In most instances, electroplated goods received special marks to identify them as such. The usual marks for plated wares were the maker's initials. Broadhead & Atkin marked their goods ⬭B&A. Philip Ashberry and Sons eventually marked their plated goods ℙA&S. A few makers used their full name mark on plated wares. In the instances where the same marks were used for plated wares and Britannia metal wares, ELECTRO PLATE or the initials EPBM were usually included on the plated wares. However, there were instances where exactly the same marks were used for both plated and unplated goods. This area of research is extremely difficult because of the very common practice of old Britannia metal goods being silverplated subsequent to their manufacture and the existence of originally silverplated wares on which the silver has worn completely away. The originally plated wares, after the passage of time and devoid of plating, often cannot be distinguished from those wares which were never plated.

Sheffield metalsmiths, notably the cutlers, had used trade marks since the 16th century, the first known being granted in 1554. The Company of Cutlers, until the early 19th century, was the responsible body for granting and registering the use of trade marks. This responsibility was restored to the Company of Cutlers in 1883. No trade marks were used on Britannia metal goods, with one rare exception,[14] until 1861 when Philip Ashberry & Sons began to include the figure of Britannia, the ancient symbol of Britain, on Britannia metal wares. With the enactment of the protection giving Trade-Marks Registration Act of 1875, a great many of the Sheffield makers' registered trade marks from that date.

The most frequently seen mark is the trumpet and banner registered by James Dixon & Sons in October, 1879. Others frequently seen are marks registered by Thomas Otley & Sons (mechanical man), James Deakin & Sons (lamp) and Walker & Hall (pennant flag with W & H, used principally on plated goods).

[14]The pair of spoons by Dixon & Son, c. 1830, mentioned in Chapter III, bear a trumpet and banner mark which was revived and registered by Dixon in 1879.

The word PATENT is seen on 19th century goods also. Inventors were granted time limited protection for their inventions as well as the right to license out their inventions to other manufacturers. In many instances the word PATENT means, that the maker produced the article under license from the inventor. The patents quite often referred to machinery used in the manufacturing process and not necessarily to some aspect of the article itself. A good example of James Shaw's patent of 1844 which related to complicated machinery for the production of oval dishes and dish covers. Many of Shaw & Fisher's hot water dishes and covers from 1844-1850 are marked with special marks referring to the patent.

One of the most interesting marks to be found on 19th century English goods of all classes are Design Registration marks. The design laws were passed to give three years exclusive right to the creator of the design. These protections came at a time when a supply of constantly new and fresh designs seemed to be imperative to the manufacturer who wanted to keep abreast of things. A drawing of the item to be registered had to be submitted, rather than a discription, and the researcher of today can refer directly to the old registration books and see the original engraving of the article registered.

The most familiar of the registration marks is the diamond with coded letters and numbers in the corners. The numbers and letters indicate the date, month and year of registration. The diamond registration mark was used from 1842 until 1883. The first registration act was passed however, in 1839 and these are identified on goods by the mark: v R REGISTERED and the number issued by the registration office. In 1842 the act was revised and the diamond mark was instituted. In 1843 a third act provided for protection of useful designs. In 1868 the letter and number codes were changed and at the end of the year 1883, the diamond and its codes were eliminated. From 1884 all registrations were indicated by R^d and the number.

Design registration marks obviously were used on goods during the first three years after being registered and often lingered on for as long as seven or eight years after the registration date.

The placing of the name of the country of origin on goods imported into the United States was the result of a requirement of the American tariff law of 1891. Many English firms then added the word ENGLAND to all their wares, for they could not always determine the final disposition of their wares. Hence, we still find many old wares in England with that country's name on the goods, even though they remained at home.

Conversely, the lack of the word ENGLAND does not necessarily mean pre-1891, for there were firms not involved in export and they had no need to use the mark.

During this period, the American tariff laws were under constant revision and in 1909 a change in the law required the additional words "MADE IN". The English manufacturers correspondingly changed their marks and from 1910 goods were marked MADE IN ENGLAND.

In the 20th century and particularly after World War I, the maker's name was often eliminated from goods which were then identified only by a trade mark

VICTORIAN DESIGN REGISTRATION MARKS

1842 - 1867	1868 - 1883

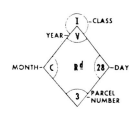

Year Letter at the top	Year Letter in the right corner

1842 - 1867	1868 - 1883
A - 1845 N - 1864	A - 1871 L - 1882
B - 1858 O - 1862	C - 1870 P - 1877
C - 1844 P - 1851	*D - 1878 S - 1875
D - 1852 Q - 1866	E - 1881 U - 1874
E - 1855 R - 1861	F - 1873 V - 1876
F - 1847 S - 1849	H - 1869 *W - 1878
G - 1863 T - 1867	I - 1872 X - 1868
H - 1843 U - 1848	J - 1880 Y - 1879
I - 1846 V - 1850	K - 1883
J - 1854 W - 1865	
K - 1857 X - 1842	*D and W used in 1878.
L - 1856 Y - 1853	
M - 1859 Z - 1860	

Month - left corner	Month - bottom corner
A - December K - November (and	A - December K - November
B - October December of 1860)	B - October M - June
*C - January M - June	*C - January *O - January
D - September *O - January	D - September R - August
E - May R - August (and Sep-	E - May W - March
G - February tember 1-19, 1857)	G - February
H - April W - March	H - April
I - July	I - July

*C and O used in January.   *C and O used in January.

DESIGN REGISTRATION NUMBERS 1884-1901

Rd. No. 1 registered January 1884	Rd. No. 205240 registered January 1893
Rd. No. 19754 registered January 1885	Rd. No. 224720 registered January 1894
Rd. No. 40480 registered January 1886	Rd. No. 246975 registered January 1895
Rd. No. 64520 registered January 1887	Rd. No. 268392 registered January 1896
Rd. No. 90483 registered January 1888	Rd. No. 291241 registered January 1897
Rd. No. 116648 registered January 1889	Rd. No. 311658 registered January 1898
Rd. No. 141273 registered January 1890	Rd. No. 331707 registered January 1899
Rd. No. 163767 registered January 1891	Rd. No. 351202 registered January 1900
Rd. No. 185713 registered January 1892	Rd. No. 368154 registered January 1901

or BEST ENGLISH PEWTER. Pattern numbers continued to be used on 20th century pewter.

After World War II, and especially after 1960, nearly all the pewter made in Sheffield has been intended for export and goods are currently made for large exporters who, in turn, ship to distributors, each of whom is identified by one or more trade names. These trade names are usually of distinct English flavor. Hence, a single manufacturer will produce thousands of tankards of the same or similar design which are distributed under a variety of trade names, none of which clearly identify the original maker.

CHAPTER SEVEN
Illustrations

ILLUSTRATIONS

As mentioned in the preface, the illustrations given here are intended to show, not only the wide variety of wares produced by the Sheffield makers for over two hundred years, but also to show those items which may generally be available to collectors and dealers.

No effort was made to edit the goods, or to select only "the best", but rather, as many items as possible were photographed. Hence, some items are pictured as found and a few snapshots of lesser photographic quality were included in the absence of professional photos.

Although much of the fine collection of the Sheffield Museum is included, the intention is not to dwell on museum collections, but to emphasize what has recently been available to collectors.

The bulk of the examples are from the author's own collection, all of which were purchased during the period 1968-1980. Other examples were photographed from dealers' stock and no doubt are now in private collections. A concluding note lists those items which are known to have been made but of which no photographs are available.

TEA AND COFFEE WARES

Coffee and tea were introduced into England during the middle of the 17th century. It would seem that coffee pre-dated tea, for the first coffee house appeared in a London advertisement of 1652, whereas the first mention of tea in England appeared in 1658, being available at the *Sultaness Head Cophee House*. The first known introduction of coffee in America was a license to serve the beverage issued in Boston in 1670. The origin of the word coffee is obscure with probable roots stemming from the Arabic qahwah.

The word tea comes from the Chinese dialect word t'e, pronounced "tay". The English originally used the "tay" pronunciation, but eventually began to use the Dutch form of "tee". The word caddy, used for small containers for the tea leaves, comes from the Chinese word for pound-*catty*.

In the 18th century, tea and coffee drinking became well established in England and America, tea being more popular in 18th century America than coffee. By the end of the 18th century and during the 19th century, taking tea became a ritual, especially in England. The extensiveness and influence of tea drinking is evidenced in antique shops where a great number of articles related to tea and coffee are offered for sale. Tea kettles, tea pots, coffee pots, sugar basins, waste bowls, cups, saucers, plates, jugs, spoons, tongs, crushers, caddies, etc., are offered in abundance, dating from the latter part of the 17th century to the present. The wares used included those made of silver, plated silver, pewter, earthenware, porcelain, glass, treen, copper, brass and iron.

It is probable that James Vickers produced teapots in white metal shortly after his establishment in 1769.

Matched tea services were unusual in the 18th century when teapots and coffee pots were made individually. The sugar basins and cream jugs were often used for other table uses in addition to tea and were not generally made to match the teapot until the final years of the century, c. 1795-1800.

From the beginning of the 19th century, in keeping with economic growth, the concept of tea services with matching pieces developed. By 1830, services included a coffee pot, teapot, hot water pot or jug, cream jug, waste bowl, and a sugar basin. In some instances, the tea caddy was also made in the same pattern. These large matched services were especially popular in America.

Tea and coffee pots were made in various capacities, measured by the half-pint. Occasionally the measurement was by the gill (¼ pint). Sizes for teapots ranged from one to eight half-pints, the most popular size being five half pints. The smallest became known as bachelor teapots. A unique bachelor teapot by Shaw & Fisher (see fig.) is the smallest teapot known, holding only half of a half pint.

During the period c.1800-1850, sugar basins were often covered and were quite large, usually the same size as the waste bowl. Sugar came to the housewife

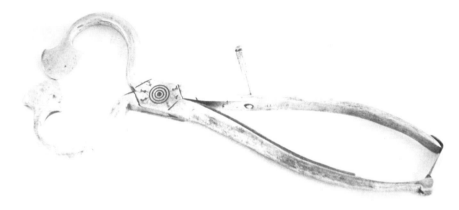

Fig. 58 Steel sugar nippers, 8 inches in length. Many nippers, which were used to cut off pieces of sugar from a cone shaped loaf, were made in Sheffield.

Fig. 59 Glass sugar crushers, about 4½ inches long, were used to help the peices of sugar dissolve in the tea cup.

in a large cone shaped loaf. In the kitchen, small chunks of sugar were cut off with sugar nippers, these chunks or lumps were served from the sugar basin with sugar tongs. The sugar, when placed in the coffee or tea was helped to dissolve by the use of a glass sugar crusher. Sugar crushers are sometimes found in metal. Finely crushed sugar was placed in castors and was shaken over food but was not used for tea or coffee. From about c. 1850 the sugar basin became smaller and less frequently covered.

Waste bowls, originally referred to as slop basins, were used to collect the tea leaves left in the bottom of the cup after the tea had been consumed. Before the pouring of a second cup of tea, the leaves were dumped into the waste bowl, leaving the cup clear for the next cup of tea. The waste bowl fell into gradual disuse after c. 1850.

The Chinese used milk or cream in their tea from ancient times and the practice was taken up by the English. The cream jug was essential to tea and coffee. Hot water jugs contained either hot water or warm milk for diluting the tea which was made quite strong.

Coffee percolators, spirit kettles and tea urns were widely produced in Sheffield Plate, silver and copper during the first half of the 19th century, but received limited use in Britannia metal and examples are not frequently found.

The percolator was basically a teapot which could be converted into a coffee pot by adding an extra part with a strainer for holding the coffee grounds. Hot water was poured over the grounds much in the same manner as the modern drip coffee pot. By removing the percolator part, and using the same lid, the pot could be used as a teapot.

Spirit kettles for tea or coffee rested on a stand over an alcohol or spirit flame which kept the contents warm.

Tea urns, although popular in other metals from the 18th century, did not appear in Britannia metal until about 1825. They, like the spirit kettles and percolators did not enjoy wide acceptance despite their good design and workmanship.

Tea extractors were known to have been in use during the period 1830-1860. Extractors were shaped somewhat like a large mustard pot with a wooden handle. Their exact use is not clearly understood.

Fig. 60 (Right) English pine dresser, c. 1820, with household wares common to the late 18th and early 19th centuries.

Fig. 61 Sugar basin by JAMES VICKERS, c.1780. Mark No. 466 *Charles V. Swain*

Fig. 62 Teapot in Adam style by JAMES VICKERS, c. 1780. Mark No. 466

Fig. 63 Tea caddy by JAMES VICKERS, c. 1790. Mark No. 467. *Katherine Ebert.*

Fig. 64 Cream jug by JAMES VICKERS, c. 1785-1795. Mark No. 467. *Charles V. Swain.*

Fig. 65 Tall coffee pot by JAMES VICKERS, c. 1785-1795. Mark No. 467.

Fig. 66 Tea caddy in Adam style with divided compartment, lock, green pineapple knob, hinged lid and bright cut engraving. RICHARD CONSTANTINE, c. 1795. Mark No. 112. *Sheffield Museum*

Fig. 67 Tea caddy in Adam style with green ivory knob, lock, hinged lid and bright cut engraving. Unmarked, c. 1790-1795. *Sheffield Museum*

Fig. 68 Teapot with applied edge, copies from contemporary Sheffield Plate by (HENRY) Froggatt, c. 1815. Mark No. 185.

Fig. 69 Teapot by I. VICKERS, c.1815-1820. Mark No. 437.

Fig. 70 Teapot by DIXON & SMITH, c.1811. Mark No. 146. *Sheffield Museum.*

Fig. 71 Teapot by DIXON & SMITH, c.1815. Mark No. 147.

105

Fig. 72 Teapot by DIXON & SMITH, c. 1812-1815. Mark No. 146.

Fig. 73 Teapot by DIXON & SMITH, c. 1815-1820. Mark No. 146.

Fig. 74 Teapot by DIXON & SMITH, c. 1815-1822. Mark No. 147.

106

Fig. 75 Teapot by (WILLIAM) PARKIN, c. 1815. Mark No. 353.

Fig. 76 Cream jug by (WILLIAM) PARKIN, c.1814-1820. Mark No. 353.

Fig. 77 Sugar basin by I. VICKERS, c.1810. Mark No. 467. Note the bottom is a separate piece and that the rim has an applied edge. *Sheffield Museum.*

Fig. 78 Teapot by DIXON
& SMITH, c. 1818.

Fig. 79 Large tea or coffee pot by DIXON & SON, c.1828. Mark No. 147. *Zera L. Hair.*

Fig.80 Bachelor size teapot by I. VICKERS, c.1815. The globular shape introduced about 1815, was popular throughout the 19th century. Constructed of two halves, the rings helped to conceal the seam. Mark No. 467. *Sheffield Museum.*

Fig. 81 Bachelor size teapot. Unmarked, c.1810-1825.

Fig. 82 Bachelor size teapot by DIXON & SON, c.1825. Mark No. 147.

Fig. 83 Tea or coffee pot
by DIXON & SMITH, c. 1818.

Fig. 84 Sugar and creamer by ARMITAGES & STANDISH, c.1829. Mark No. 10. The cream
jug at first glance would seem to be a bachelor teapot but metal handles were never used on
teapots prior to 1840, and closer inspection reveals that the spout opens directly into the body
of the jug, having no grate or strainer as a teapot would have.

110

Fig. 85 Tea caddy by DIXON & SON, with hinged lid, lock and key, 1823-1829. Mark No. 147.

Fig. 87 Cream jug by DIXON & SON, 1823-1829. Mark No. 147.

Fig. 86 Covered sugar by DIXON & SON, 1823-1829. Mark No. 147.

111

Fig. 88 Sugar, cream and tea caddy of matching style of DIXON & SON, 1823-1829. Mark No. 147.

Fig. 89 Sugar (lid missing) by DIXON & SON, 1823-1829. Mark No. 147.

Fig. 90 Cream jug by DIXON & SON, 1823-1829. Mark No. 147.

Fig. 91 Sugar and creamer by DIXON & SON, 1823-1829. Mark No. 147.

Fig. 92 Teapot by DIXON &
SON, 1823-1829. Mark
No. 147

Fig. 93 Coffee pot by
DIXON & SON, 1823-
1829. Mark No. 147

113

Fig. 94 Coffee Pot by DIXON & SON, c. 1828-1829. A very early appearance of the panneled shape. Mark No. 147

Fig. 95 (Right) DIXON & SON, c. 1829, Mark No. 147.

114

Fig. 96 Tea and coffee service by DIXON & SON, c. 1829. Coffee pot, teapot, hot water pot, waste bowl, covered sugar and covered cream jog. Complete services prior to 1830 are very rare. Mark No. 147.

116

Fig. 97 Teapot by I. VICKERS with filled silver knnob, c. 1830. Mark No. 467

Fig. 98 Teapot JAMES DIXON & SON, c. 1830 with filled silver knob. Mark No. 149

Fig. 99 Coffee pot by R. BROADHEAD, 1830-1833. Mark No. 78.

Fig. 100 Tea service by JAMES DIXON & SONS, c. 1835. This style is typical of the services exported to America. Mark No. 151.

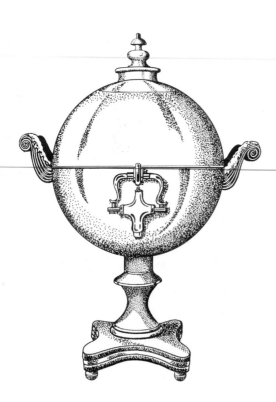

Fig. 101 Three tea urns by JOHN VICKERS. The two at the top date 1830-1835, while the one illustrated at the bottom left, dates from about 1810-1835. *Sheffield Museum.*

120

Fig. 102 Three large coffee pots, 13 inches tall, originally part of complete 5 and 6 piece coffee and tea services which were particularly popular in America during the period 1835-1845. The knob on the pot on the right is not original. JAMES DIXON & SONS, 1835-1841. (The coffee pot on the bottom dates 1840-1841). Mark No. 151.

121

Fig. 103 Coffee pot by Broadhead & Atkin, c.1843. Mark No. 85. *Sheffield Museum.*

Fig. 104 Coffee pot by WEBSTER & JOHNSONS, c.1845. Mark No. 492.

Fig. 105 Coffee pot with anti caloric handle and filled silver knob by BROADHEAD & ATKIN, 1841-1842. Mark No. 84.

Fig. 106 Coffee pot with silver filbert knob (fruit missing) by G. (George) KITCHING, 1837-1845. Mark No. 278.

122

Fig. 107 Coffee pot constructed entirely of cast pieces by BROADHEAD & ATKIN, c. 1841.
Knob not original. Mark No. 84.

Fig. 108 Coffee pot by
JAMES DIXON & SONS,
C. 1840. Mark No. 151.

Fig. 109 Teapot by JAMES
DIXON & SONS, the design
registered in 1841. Mark
No. 152

124

BACHELOR SIZE TEAPOTS

Fig. 110 J. WOLSTENHOLME, c. 1830. Mark No. 515.

Fig. 111 JAMES DIXON & SONS, c.1835. Mark No. 151.

Fig. 112 I. VICKERS, c.1840. Mark No. 468.

Fig. 113 I. (JOHN) TYLER, c.1840. Mark No. 459.

Fig. 114 G. (GEORGE) KITCHING, c.1835. Mark No. 277.

Fig. 115 BROADHEAD & ATKIN, c.1840. Mark No. 83. *Sheffield Museum.*

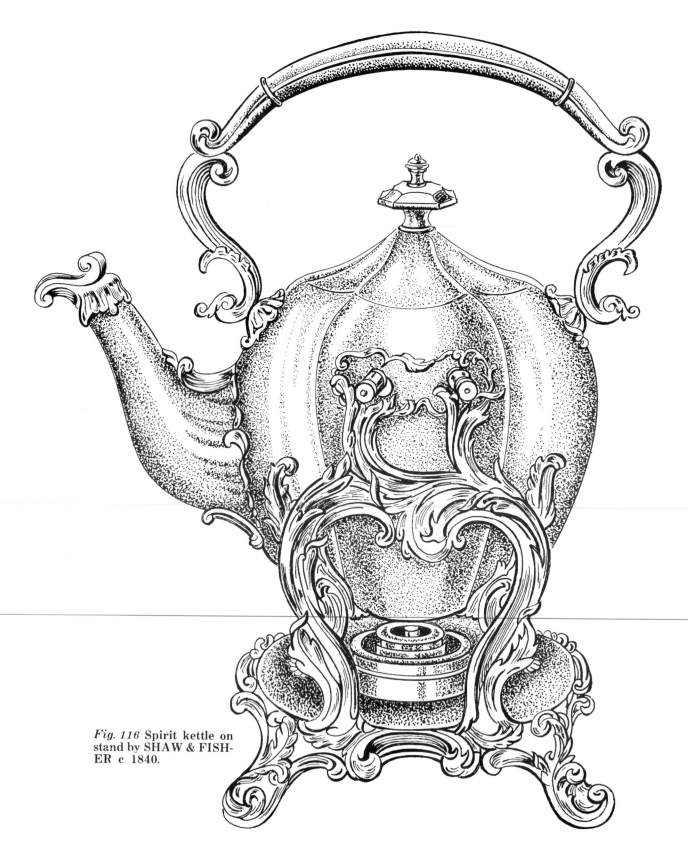

Fig. 116 Spirit kettle on stand by SHAW & FISH-ER c 1840.

Fig. 117 Tea extractors were known to have been made from about 1830 to 1860. Their exact function or use is unclear. The left example from the *Sheffield Museum* is by JAMES DIXON & SONS, c.1851-c.1860, Mark No. 161 and the extractor to the right is unmarked and could date as early as 1830.

Fig. 118 Sugar and creamer with colbalt blue ceramic liners by BROADHEAD & ATKIN, c.1845. Mark No. 86. *Sheffield Museum.*

Fig. 120 Cream jug with colbalt blue ceramic liner by BROADHEAD & ATKIN, c.1845. Mark No. 86.

Fig. 119 Cream jug by JAMES DIXON & SONS, 1835-1841. Mark No. 151.

Fig. 121 Teapot by SHAW & FISHER, c. 1842. Mark No. 417.

Fig. 122 Teapot by T. (THOMAS) PARKIN, with filled silver knob, c.1838. Mark No. 357.

Fig. 123 Cream jug by T. (Thomas) Parkin, c.1838. This cream jug is a companion to the teapot illustrated in Fig.   .Mark No. 356.

128

REGISTERED DESIGNS BY SHAW & FISHER
(Sheffield Central Library)

Fig. 124 May 13, 1843

Fig. 125 May 13, 1843

Fig. 126 October 17, 1843

Fig. 127 April 4, 1844

Fig. 128 May 2, 1845

Fig. 129 Coffee pot registered by JAMES DIXON & SONS, Jan. 29, 1850. Knob not original. Mark No. 159.

Fig. 130 Teapot, companion to the coffee pot illustrated in Fig. 129. Registered Jan. 29, 1850, by JAMES DIXON & SONS.

Fig. 131 Unique melon teapot registered by JAMES DIXON & SONS, July 1848.

Fig. 132 Teapot "Published By" BROAD-HEAD & ATKIN, 1846. Mark No. 87.

Fig. 133 This is not trick photography. The mini pot is marked ½ of a half pint and is shown with a regular size tea cup of the same period. In addition to the capacity mark, other marks include the pattern number and the maker, SHAW & FISHER. c1845. Mark No. 417.

Fig. 134 Half pint coffee pot by JAMES DIXON & SONS, 1842-1851. Mark No. 157.

Fig. 135 Teapot with filled silver knob, by SHAW & FISHER, c.1845. Mark No. 417.

Fig. 136 Teapot by BROADHEAD & ATKIN, c. 1850. Mark No. 86. The horizontal body seam indicates that this round teapot was made in two halves even thoug spinning had been introduced some 25 years earlier.

Fig. 137 Teapot by R. BROADHEAD & CO., c.1855. The knob is a replacement. Mark No. 90.

Fig. 138 Teapot by JAMES ALLAN & CO., c.1850. The metal knob is in the style of the filled silver knobs of c.1830. Mark No. 4.

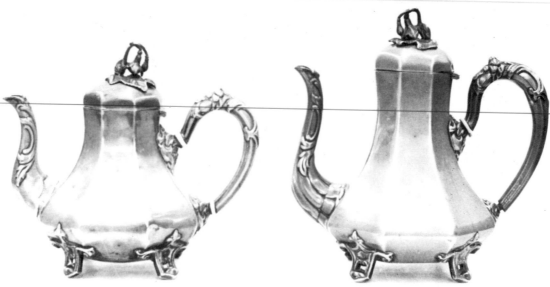

Fig. 139 Teapot and matching coffee pot by J. (Jospeh) BROWN, c. 1850. Mark No. 97.

Fig. 140 teapot by BROADHEAD & ATKIN, c. 1850. Mark No. 86.

Fig. 141 Teapot, similar to Fig. 140, with the same spout, feet and handle, by BROADHEAD & ATKIN. c.1850. Mark No. 86.

Fig. 142 Teapot by THOMAS PARKIN, c. 1845, MarkNo. 358.

Fig. 143 Teapot by BROADHEAD & ATKIN. c.1845.

133

Fig. 144 Bachelor size teapot by JAMES DIXON & SONS, c. 1850. Mark No. 157. *Zair L. Hair.*

Fig. 145 Bachelor size teapot, by SAM'L RUSSELL, c. 1845-1849. Mark No. 401.

Fig. 146 Bachelor size teapot by RICHARD PARKIN & SONS, c. 1855-1860. Mark No. 360.

Fig. 147 Teapot by PHILIP ASHBERRY & SONS, c. 1861. Marks No. 36 and 37.

Fig. 148 Cream jug, BROADHEAD & ATKIN, c. 1850. Mark No. 86.

Fig. 149 Cream jug, Unmarked, c. 1860.

Fig. 150 Teapot by JAMES DIXON & SONS, c.1842-1845, Mark No. 157. This and the teapot in Fig. 151 were two of many designs copied by the American makers, Reed & Barton.

Fig. 151 Teapot by JAMES DIXON & SONS, c. 1842-1845. Knob not original Mark No. 157.

Fig. 152 Teapot by SHAW & FISHER, c. 1855-c. 1860. Mark No. 417.

Fig. 153 Teapot by E. STACEY & SON, c. 1860. Mark No. 439.

Fig. 154 Coffee pot by F. J. FOWLER, c.1850. Mark No. 182. *Sheffield Museum.*

Fig. 155 Coffee pot by PHILIP ASHBERRY, c.1850-1855. Mark No. 27.

Fig. 156 Teapot by LAND, c.1865. This style is much more characteristic of the period 1845-1850. Mark No. 279.

Fig. 157 Teapot by PHILIP ASHBERRY & SONS, c.1856-1860. This teapot was originally electroplated and is marked with Ashberry's early electroplate mark. Mark No. 33.

Fig. 158 Teapot by PHILIP ASHBERRY & Sons, c. 1860. Marks No 32 and No. 35.

Fig. 159 Teapot by SHAW & FISHER, c.1860. Mark No. 417.

Fig. 160 Teapot by ATKIN BROTHERS, c.1860. Mark No. 43.

Fig. 161 Teapot by BROADHEAD & CO., c.1860. Mark No. 93.

Fig. 162 Teapot by I. (JOHN) TYLER, Fruit missing from knob, c.1865. Mark No. 459.

Fig. 163 Teapot by E. STACEY & SON, c.1860. Mark No. 439.

137

Fig. 164 Coffee pot by PHILIP ASHBERRY & SONS, c. 1865. Mark No. 37.

Fig. 165 Coffee pot, 12 inches tall by JAMES DIXON & SONS, with *patent non conductor* handle. c. 1860. Marks No. 32 and 161.

Fig. 166 Coffee pot by JAMES DIXON & SONS, c. 1870. Mark No. 161.

Fig. 167 Coffee pot by JOSPEH DEAKIN & SONS, c. 1865. Mark No. 137.

138

Fig. 168 One of a very few dated teapots. The close ups show the fine detail of the cast feet, electroplated knob and engraving. JAMES DIXON & SONS, 1865. Mark No. 161.

139

Fig. 169 Teapot, originally silver plated, by PHILIP ASHBERRY & SONS, c.1865, Mark No. 33.

Fig. 170 Teapot by E. STACEY & SON, c.1860. Mark No. 439.

Fig. 171 Teapot by JAMES DIXON & SONS, c.1865. Mark No. 161.

Fig. 172 Teapot by JAMES DIXON & SONS, c.1885. Mark No. 164. This same design is illustrated in Fig. 171 with a wooden handle.

140

Fig. 173 Three views of a percolator by JOSEPH RIDGE & CO., c. 1881-1884. Mark No. 389. Percolators were in essence, drip coffee makers which could be converted to a teapot. Their greatest popularity was 1810-1830. The appearance of one in 1881-1884 is unusual. (A) The complete percolator (B) The coffee container removed (C) A teapot.

*Fig.*174 Teapot by JAMES ALLAN, c. 1870. The knob, a replacement, is nearly identical to the original. Mark No. 5.

Fig. 175   Teapot by WOLSTENHOLME & BIGGIN, 1876-1879. Mark No. 518. *Sheffield Museum.*

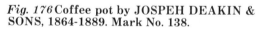

Fig. 176 Coffee pot by JOSPEH DEAKIN & SONS, 1864-1889. Mark No. 138.

Fig. 177 Teapot by JOSEPH DEAKIN & SONS, c. 1860. Mark No. 136. *Sheffield Museum.*

142

Fig. 178 Three typical Adam revival teapots, c. 1870-c. 1880. The top two are unmarked, the bottom one made by JOHN NODDER & SONS. Mark No. 320.

143

Fig. 179 Typical Adam revival teapots of the 1880-1920 period. The teapot on the top was made by E. STACEY & SON, c. 1890., Mark No. 439. The other two were originally electroplated and carry no maker's name. The insert shows the hand engraving which had beginnings in the 18th century and continued throughout the 19th and into the 20th century.

144

Fig. 180 Tea pot by THOMAS OTLEY & SONS, c. 1880. Mark No. 338.

Fig. 181 Teapot by JAMES DIXON & SONS, c. 1880. Mark No. 164. This design is more characteristic of 1860 than 1880. *Dorothy Boyce.*

Fig. 182 Teapot by SHAW & FISHER, c. 1870. Mark no. 417.

Fig. 183 Teapot by M. HUNTER & SONS, c. 1885. Mark No. 262.

Fig. 184 Teapot by JOSEPH DEAKIN & SONS, c. 1880, Mark No. 137.

Fig. 185 Teapot by ABRAM BROOKSBANK, c. 1885. Mark No. 93.

145

Fig. 186 Patented self pouring tea pot by JAMES DIXON & SONS, c. 1886, (knob missing). An air tight shaft connected to the lid causes a vaccuum when the lid is lifted, releasing the tea out the spout. Mark No. 165.

Fig. 187 Patented self pouring teapot by JAMES DIXON & SONS. The feature was incorporated in different designs. c. 1886. Mark No. 165.

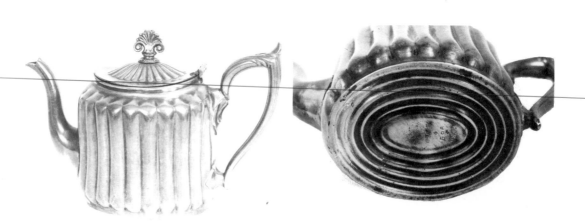

Fig. 188 In August, 1889, PHILIP ASHBERRY applied for a patent to protect his use of expansion bottom teapots. Patent No. 13,360 was granted in April, 1890. This teapot, originally electroplated and marked EXPANSION BOTTOM, was made by PHILIP ASHBERRY, c. 1890, Mark No. 33.

Fig. 189 **Embossed electroplated coffee pot unmarked, c. 1880. These embossed designs were peculiar to electro plated wares and were almost never used on unplated Britannia metal.**

Fig. 190 Coffee pot, unmarked, c. 1890.

Fig. 191 Teapot by JAMES DIXON & SONS, c. 1890-1900. Mark No. 164.

Fig. 192 Patented teapot with heat relieving handle and a hinged, swinging grate by WALKER & HALL, c. 1890. Mark No. 475.

147

Fig. 193 Teapot by JAMES DIXON & SONS, 1903, with a quaint engraved inscription. Mark No. 164.

Fig. 194 Partial tea service made by an **unidentified Sheffield marker for Hamilton Laidlaw, Glasgow, c. 1935. Mark No. 244.** *Boone's Antiques*

Fig. 195 Tea service marked PERIOD PEWTER, the trade mark for Frank Cobb, c. 1920-1939. Mark No. 111. *Boone's Antiques*

149

Fig. 196 Modern tea wares by WARDLE & MATTHEWS, LTD, c. 1970++.

Fig. 197 Modern coffee and tea service by JAMES DIXON & SONS, c. 1950-1970.

Fig. 198 Pierced salt (blue glass liner missing) by JAMES VICKERS, c. 1790. Mark No. 467. *Charles V. Swain.*

Fig. 199 Blue lined salt, unmarked, c. 1830-1835.

Fig. 200 Blue lined salt by SHAW & FISHER, c. 1835-1840. *Sheffield Central Library.*

Fig. 201 Pierced salt with blue glass liner, c. 1850, unmarked.

Fig. 202 Salt by JAMES DIXON & SONS, c. 1855, having a blue glass liner with a finely ground pontil. Mark No. 161.

Fig. 203 Salt with earthenware blue liner missing. Although of a style c. 1820, the mark indicates a date of c. 1910. W. HUTTON & SONS. Mark No. 263.

Fig. 204 Three typical 19th century lion footed salts, unmarked, as they always are in the 19th century. Difficult to date but probably made from about 1850++.

Fig. 205 Pepper pots are often difficult to date. On the left, c. 1850; second from the left, c. 1810-1820; second from the right, c. 1845. All unmarked. *Sheffield Museum.*

Fig. 206 These might fool the unsuspecting collector. Careful inspection will show the peppers to be made entirely of lead and originally cheaply electroplated, the silver now worn away. c. 1870-1900.

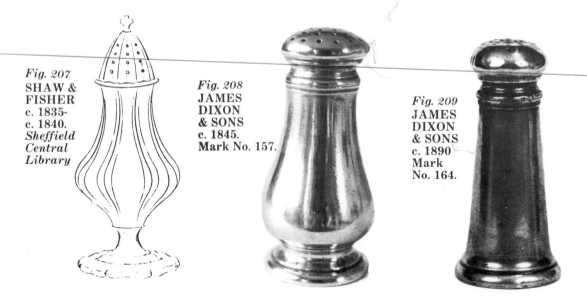

Fig. 207
SHAW &
FISHER
c. 1835-
c. 1840.
*Sheffield
Central
Library*

Fig. 208
JAMES
DIXON
& SONS
c. 1845.
Mark No. 157.

Fig. 209
JAMES
DIXON
& SONS
c. 1890
Mark
No. 164.

152

Fig. 210 Mustard pot by DIXON & SON, c. 1825. Mark No. 147. *Sheffield Museum.*

Fig. 211 Mustard pot by SHAW & FISHER, c. 1835-1840. *Sheffield Central Library.*

Fig. 212 Pierced mustard pot with removeable colbalt blue glass liner, c. 1850. Unmarked.

Fig. 213 Mustard pot with removeable colbalt glass liner, by JAMES DIXON & SONS, c. 1845. Mark No. 151. This pattern was very popular, being produced by DIXON and others in silver and Old Sheffield Plate. It also appears with later DIXON Marks. No. 157 and No. 161.

Fig. 214 Mustard pot with removeable glass liner by PHILIP ASHBERRY & SONS, c. 1856-1860. Mark No. 29.

Fig. 215 Two unmarked mustard pots in which the metal is spun directly to the colbalt blue earthenware liners. Both produced c. 1850, although the design of the pot on the left is c. 1840 and the right c. 1810.

Fig. 216 Three piece, hot water covered steak dish with wooden bun feet by DIXON & SON, c. 1825. Mark No. 147.

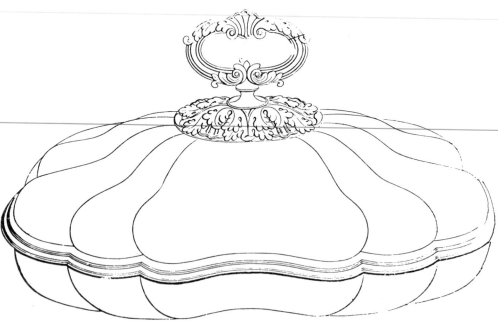

Fig. 217 Covered steak dish with filled silver handle by SHAW & FISHER, c. 1840. *Sheffield Central Library.*

154

Fig. 218 Double dish by SHAW & FISHER. The handle twists out so that the top becomes a serving dish. c. 1835. *Sheffield Central Library.*

Fig. 219 Hot water covered dish by HENRY WILKINSON, registered November, 1845.

Fig. 220 Pair of hot water plates with gadroon edges by DIXON & SON, 1823-1829, Mark No. 147.

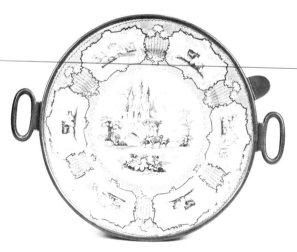

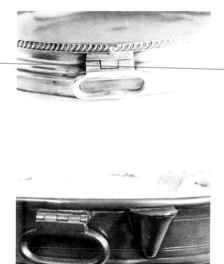

Fig. 221 Hot water plate by I. VICKERS, combined with a green transfer earthenware plate, c. 1842. Mark No. 469.

Fig. 222 Large hot water venison dish by ATKIN BROTHERS, c. 1860. Mark no. 43.

Fig. 223 Large hot water venison dish, 23" across the handles, with Japanned wood handles and bun feet, JAMES DIXON & SONS, c. 1835. Mark. No. 151.

157

Fig. 224 Dish cover registered by JAMES DIXON & SONS, August 31, 1877. The mark includes the trumpet and banner registered in 1879, dating the cover about 1879-1880. Mark No. 164.

Fig. 225 Dish Cover, 12 inches, by JAMES DIXON & SONS, c. 1885. Mark No. 164.

Fig. 226 Set of Dish Covers registered by JAMES DIXON & SONS, September 6, 1848. The mark indicates that this set was made after 1851, probably c. 1855. The insert shows the detail of the silver filled handle. Mark No. 161.

Fig. 227 Gravy spoon,
12½ inches long by
(HENRY) FROGGATT,
c. 1795. Mark 184.

Fig. 228 Tea spoons and tablespoons by
ASHBERRY. The two teaspoons date c.
1860, Mark No. 28 and the tablespoons date
c. 1840-1860 with Marks No. 23 and 25.

Fig. 229 Pair of tablespoons
by DIXON & SON, c. 1830.
Mark No. 150.

Fig. 230 Tablespoon by
PHILIP ASHBERRY, 1829.
Mark No. 14.

Fig. 231 Tablespoon, 1836-
1839 by I. PEARCE, Mark
No. 369.

160

Fig. 232 Ladle by DIXON & SON, 1823-1829. Mark No. 147.

Fig. 233 Ladle by PHILIP ASHBERRY, c. 1830. Mark No. 17.

Fig. 234 Ladle by J. (JOSEPH) CUTTS, 1841-1852. Mark No. 126.

Fig. 235 Pair of sauce ladles by PHILIP ASHBERRY, 1830-1836. Mark No. 19.

Fig. 236 Sauce boat, c. 1820. Unmarked. *Sheffield Museum.*

161

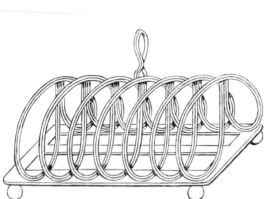

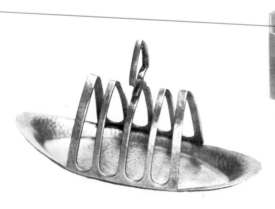

Fig. 238 Toast rack by Philip Ashberry, c. 1845. Mark No. 26.

Fig. 237 Toast rack, c. 1840.

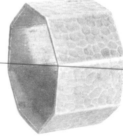

Fig. 240 Serviette rings made by George Lee
& Co. and marked MY LADY, c. 1935. Mark
No. 292.

Fig. 239 Hand hammered toast rack, unmarked, c. 1930.

Fig. 241 Large oval tray, from a tea service by COOPER BROTHERS AND SONS, LTD., c. 1926-1939. Marks No. 114 and 115. *Boone's Antiques.*

Fig. 242 Round, hammered tray marked CRAFTSMAN, by Viner's Ltd., c. 1935. Mark No 474.

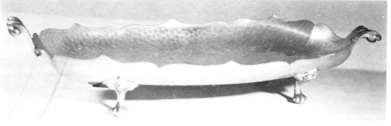

Fig. 243 Relish dish produced from 1935 to 1968 by JAMES DIXON & SONS. Mark No. 166. *Boone's Antiques*

163

Fig. 244 Claret jug by JAMES VICKERS with bright cut engraving. Height 13" to the top of the knob. c. 1785-1795. Mark No. 467. *James B. Laughlin*

Fig. 245 A Trellis Jug made at the Staffordshire pottery owned by Charles Meigh and registered on September 18, 1848. May jugs were purchased unlidded from the potteries and delivered to Sheffield makers where they were mounted with metal lids and then sold to the public. This potter's mark, shown at the right is moulded on the bottom of the jug and the incised mark of BROADHEAD & ATKIN, who made and mounted the lid, is located on the inside of the lid. Mark No. 88.

Fig. 246 Typical lidded jug, c. 1840-1850. Unmarked.

Fig. 247 Jug, c. 1850. Unmarked.

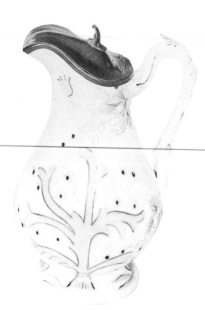

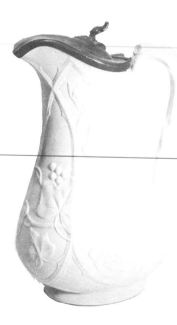

Fig. 248 Colorful lidded jub, one of a pair, the other of which is unlidded and dated 1851. Unmarked.

Fig. 249 Lidded jug registered by the potter, WILLIAM BROWN-FIELD, April 10, 1856. The lid is unmarked.

Fig. 250 Adam revival jug, c. 1870-1880. Unmarked.

Fig. 251 Ice water jug with an inner lining by ATKIN BROTHERS. The lid is missing, c. 1880. Mark No. 43. *Boone's Antiques*

Fig. 252 Jug by PHILIP ASBHERRY & SONS, c. 1880. Mark No. 37. *Boone's Antiques*

Fig. 253 Jug with stag horn handle by JAMES DIXON & SONS, c. 1885. Mark No. 164. *Boone's Antiques.*

167

Fig. 254 Enamel decorated earthenware milk jug and sugar basin. c. 1880. The jug is mounted with a pewter lid. Unmarked.

Fig. 255 Jackfield jug with enamel decoration. The lever action lid opens when the white porcelain button is depressed. Made by Harrison Fisher and marked TRAFALGAR, c. 1900. Mark No. 179.

Fig. 256 Hot water jug by JAMES DIXON & SONS, C. 1900. Mark No. 164.

Fig. 257 Modern beer Jugs by PEWTER MANUFACTURING CO., c. 1978++.

Fig. 258 Modern water jugs by WARDLE & MATTHEWS, c. 1973++.

Fig. 259 Gill and half gill measures by DIXON & SON with George IV Imperial escutcheons, c. 1824-1829. Marks No. 147 and 148.

Fig. 260 George IV escutcheon soldered to the DIXON & SON Measures showing the detail of the Imperial Standard Mark. The IV can be seen inside the base of the crown.

Fig. 261 Gill measure by DIXON & SON showing the great wear on the escutcheon as a result of many years of service, 1824-1829. Marks No. 147 and 148.

Fig. 262 Gill and two gill measures by DIXON & SON with George IV Imperial escutcheons and dated 1824. Marks No. 147 and 148. *Sheffield Museum.*

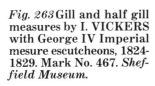

Fig. 263 Gill and half gill measures by I. VICKERS with George IV Imperial mesure escutcheons, 1824-1829. Mark No. 467. *Sheffield Museum.*

Fig. 264 Pint measure, 1824-1829, mark illegible.

171

Fig. 265 Beer jug by DIXON & SMITH, c. 1818. These jugs were made in 3 half pints, quart, 5 half pints, 3 pints and 2 quart sizes. The shape is very similar to coffee pots of the period known as "Biggins" and a notation in the catalog indicates that coffee strainers were available to accompany the jugs at an extra cost of one shilling.

Fig. 266 Lidded tankard by DIXON & SMITH, c. 1815.

172

Fig. 267 Three tankards of the same design, produced by JAMES DIXON & SONS over a span of 120 years. The quart on the left is dated 1882 and although only the retail store name is stamped on the bottom, it also includes the DIXON pattern number. In the center is a lidded pint which dates about 1860, Mark No. 161. On the right is a new lidded pint, 1980. Mark No. 166.

173

Fig. 268 Half pint tankard by JAMES DIXON & SONS, c. 1890. Mark No. 164.

Fig. 269 Glass bottomed pint tankard by JAMES DIXON & SONS, c. 1870. Mark No. 163.

Fig. 270 Pint tankard by ATKIN BROTHERS, c. 1940. Mark No. 43.

Fig. 271 Pint tankard marked MY LADY, by George Lee & Co., c. 1930. Mark No. 291.

Fig. 272 Pint tankard by Bramwell, Brownhill & Co., Marked with their trade mark, RELIABLE. c. 1925. Mark No. 68.

Fig. 273 Pint tankard marked MANOR PERIOD by Travis Wilson & Co., Ltd., c. 1930. Mark No. 452. *Boones Antiques.*

Fig. 274 Pint tankard by JAMES DIXON & SONS, c. 1940. Mark No. 166.

Fig. 275 Pint tankard marked MANOR by A. Milns & Co., c. 1925. Mark No. 314.

Fig. 276 Pint tankard by VINERS, c. 1948. Mark No. 471.

Fig. 277 Pint tankard by K. BRIGHT, 1951-1959. Mark No. 74.

Fig. 278 Pint tankard by Viners, c. 1960. Mark No. 472.

Fig. 279 The Worchester tankard was first produced by Cooper Brothers & Sons, Ltd. in 1935 and remains in production at present. This example dates c. 1970. Marks No. 115 and 116.

Fig. 280 Modern tankards by WARDLE & MATTHEWS, c. 1973++.

Fig. 281 Modern goblets by PEWTER MANUFACTURING COMPANY, c. 1978.

Fig. 282 Typical mid 19th to early 20th century dram or gin flasks. The flask itself is made of glass covered with leather and the metal bottom slips off to be used as a cup. This type of flask dates from about 1835 to 1950. The vertical window in the leather cover became popular from about 1870, although many flasks were made after the date without windows. Dram flasks were offered by many makers in a wide range of sizes.

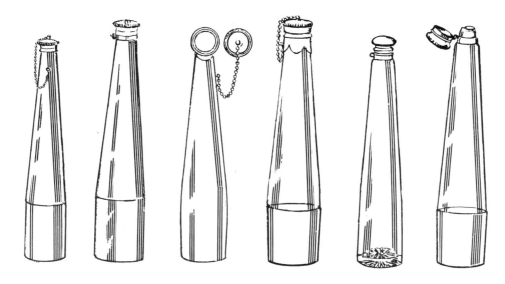

Fig. 283 Various wine flasks, some with removable cups on the bottom. These were made for hunters and sportsmen and were carried in leather cases of the same shape. JAMES DIXON & SONS, c. 1886. *Sheffield Museum.*

177

Fig. 284 All metal flask by
BUXTON & RUSSELL, c.
1852-1860. Mark No. 102

Fig. 285 Unmarked flask
with hand hammered cup
bottom, c. 1920-1939.

Fig. 286 Whiskey measure
made by JAMES DIXON &
SONS, from 1945 to the
present time. Mark No.
166.

Fig. 287 20 oz. "Just A
Thimble Full" whiskey
measure by WARDLE &
MATTHEWS. They have
been made in 2, 4, 8 and 20
oz. sizes since 1965. Thimble
measures were also made
in the late 19th century.

CANDLESTICKS

Sheffield in the 18th and 19th centuries was especially well known for silver and Sheffield Plate candlesticks. The Britannia metal makers capitalized on this popularity and produced great numbers of candlesticks and chambersticks which were either copies of those made in silver and Sheffield Plate or made in similar style. For the most part, the most popular Britannia metal sytles were those of simple, traditional forms.

Britannia metal candlesticks made in the Adam style prior to 1800 are very rare.

Nearly all of the 19th century baluster push up English pewter candlesticks which have been so popular with antique collectors were made of Britannia metal in Sheffield and Birmingham. The push up feature (from the bottom) first came into use about 1800.

For some unexplained reason the baluster candlesticks were unmarked while the chambersticks were often marked. The candlelabra popular in silver and Sheffield Plate were rarely made in Britannia metal.

Snuffers were an essential household item for trimming candle wicks. Until mid 19th century, candles did not have clean burning wicks. While lit, the wicks charred, causing the candle to burn poorly, and to make a great deal of smoke. This charred part of the wick was called snuff and had to be frequently removed with sissor like snuffers. This allowed better light and less smoke. Improved wicks were introduced about 1826, but snuffers continued in use beyond 1860. The snuffers usd with Britannia metal candlesticks were polished steel and were usually kept on a Britannia metal tray. Brass snuffers and trays were used with brass candlesticks as were Sheffield Plate and silver snuffers for those candlesticks.

Chambersticks were sold in pairs with snuffer cones and steel snuffers. Their use continued in England into the 20th century. Chambersticks of the 1810-1830 period often featured an open slot below the candle holder. This allowed a safe and handy place for the snuffers to rest.

Telescopic candlesticks were introduced by the Sheffield Plate industry in 1795 and were popular for about 20 years. To a lesser extent, they were also made in brass and in silver. Telescopic candlesticks are very rare in pewter and were seldom made after 1820.

179

Fig. 288 Pair of rare telescopic candlesticks. c. 1805. Unmarked. *Peter Thompson.*

Fig. 289 Gadroon edges were featured on candlesticks of the period 1800-1830. The gadroon was cast into the design, however, and not added separately as in other wares.

Fig. 290 Typical candlestick styles dating 1830-1860.

Fig. 291 Early Victorian candlesticks c. 1840-1870.

182

Fig. 292 Chamberstick, one of a pair, by DIXON & SMITH,
c. 1811-1822.

Fig. 293 Chambersticks by PHILIP ASHBERRY & SONS, 1856-1860. Mark No. 29.

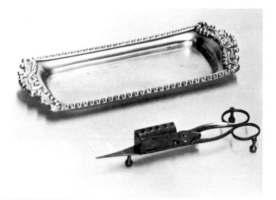

Fig. 294 Snuffer tray with the edges mounted in the style of Old Sheffield Plate by DIXON & SON, 1823-1829. Mark No. 147.

Fig. 295 Snuffer tray with gadroon edge by JAMES DIXON & SON, 1830-1834. Mark No. 149.

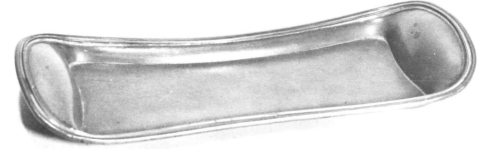

Fig. 296 Snuffer tray with thread edge by JAMES DIXON & SONS, 1842-1851. Mark No. 157.

Fig. 297 Snuffer tray by BROADHEAD & ATKIN, 1843-1853. Mark No. 86.

Fig. 298 Snuffer tray by PHILIP ASHBERRY accompanied by the original sketch submitted for registration Dec. 5, 1848. The tray is unmarked.

184

INKWELLS

Inks were used by Egyptian and Chinese cultures as early as 2500 B.C. Since that time containers were developed to hold the ink and have become known as inkwells. Hollow reeds and bamboo have been used with ink, but the quill, taken from a goose or swan proved to be the most popular writing tool of the western world.

By 1809, in England, a workable system of cutting off the end or nib of a quill and placing it on a holder was devised. The nibs were used somewhat in the same manner as the steel points that were to follow. As the quill nibs wore down they could be sharpened several times and the small knives used for this purpose became known as pen knives.

Although experiments with metal points were conducted for centuries, the widespread use of metal pen points did not occur until the middle of the 19th century. Even then, with all refinements, the steel pen points were never equal to the goose quill for smooth penmanship.

In the late 18th and early 19th century inkstands were designed to incorporate two inkwells, a pounce pot, and a storage area for quills, nibs, and wafers for sealing letters. The pounce pot contained very fine sand which was sprinkled over the aper to dry the ink. Upon drying, the sand was returned to the pounce pot. Many of these were made in Sheffield. Eventually, in the 19th century, the inkstand gave way to the more popular use of a single inkwell.

The ink was thick and sludge-like and the ink well (not the glass well which actually held the ink) was filled with fine lead shot. The shot had two purposes. It gave weight to the ink well, thereby preventing accidents, and it served as a cleaner for the pen. By pushing the pen into one of the holes in the top of the inkwell, the shot cleaned the nib of sludge.

About 1850 inkwells began to include a flat plate for a base. These were often used in commercial and public places such as the bank and pot office. The inkwells with the plate base survived well into the 20th century and had been in use as late as 1970 in English post offices and public agencies.

Inkwells were made by most of the Sheffield makers but often were unmarked.

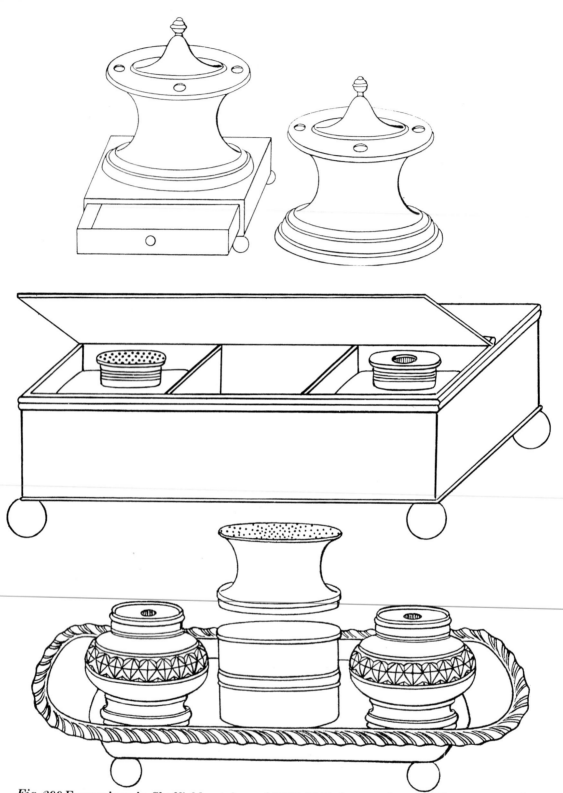

Fig. 299 Engravings in Sheffield catalogs of 1810-1845 show various writing wares such as these. Unmarked double flapped inkstands and small inkstands with drawer have here-to-fore been attributed to the work of earlier pewterers.

Fig. 300 c. 1860-c. 1870.

Fig. 301 c. 1880.

Fig. 302 JAMES DIXON & SONS,
c. 1860. Mark No. 161.

Fig. 303 c. 1860-1870.

Fig. 304 c. 1880++.

Fig. 305 Sigar (sic) case by
DIXON & SMITH, c. 1815-1822.

Fig. 306 Tobacco box with lead
weight inside. **DIXON & SON,**
1823-1829. Mark No. 147.

Fig. 307 Tobacco box, unmarked, c. 1845.

Fig. 308 Tobacco box or cistern by **SHAW**
& FISHER, c. 1845. *Sheffield Central*
Library.

Fig. 309 Tobacco box by SHAW & FISHER, c. 1845. *Sheffield Central Library.*

Fig. 310 Tobacco box by E. STACEY & SON, c. 1860. Mark No. 439. *Sheffield Museum.*

Fig. 311 Unmarked tobacco box, c. 1850.

Fig. 312 Shaving boxes by SHAW & FISHER, c. 1845. *Sheffield Central Library.*

Fig. 313 Shaving or soap box, unmarked, c. 1850.

Fig. 314 Desk tidy box, unmarked, c. 1860.

Fig. 315 Snuff box, dated 1815, unmarked.

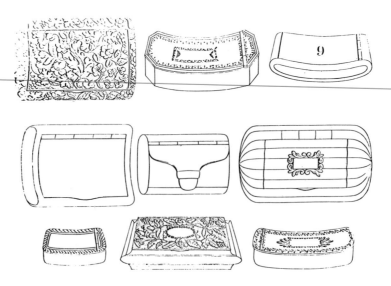

Fig. 316 Snuff boxes by SHAW & FISHER, c. 1845. *Sheffield Central Library.*

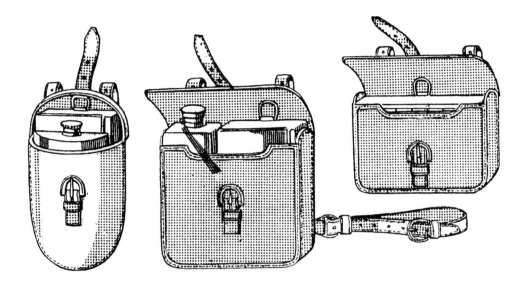

Fig. 317 Canteens or lunch boxes for sportsmen with sandwich boxes and gin or wine flasks. JAMES DIXON & SONS, c. 1880. *Sheffield Museum.*

Fig. 318 Folding sandwich box often carried in a leather holster by JAMES DIXON & SONS, c. 1880. *Sheffield Museum.*

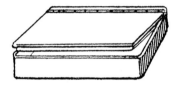

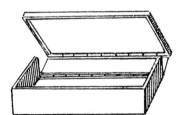

Fig. 319 Cheese box from a sportsman's canteen. JAMES DIXON & SONS, c. 1880. Mark. No. 164. *Zera L. Hair.*

191

*Fig. 320*Shaving mug by JAMES DIXON & SONS, c. 1890. Mark No. 164. A hinged lid covers the brush holder and the soap dish resting in the top of the mug lifts out.

Fig. 321 Communion flagon and paten or plate by DIXON & SON, 1823-1829. Mark No. 147.

Fig. 322 Communion chalice by I. VICKERS, c. 1800-1820. Mark No. 467. *Dorothy Boyce.*

Fig. 323 Pair of communion chalices, unmarked, c. 1800-1820. *Boone's Antiques.*

193

Fig. 324 This drawing is taken from an interesting old scrap book in the archives of the Sheffield Central Library. The notes accompanying the drawing state that the set was discovered in an old cupboard in Sheffield, in 1934, and was made and marked by I. Vickers, each piece being engraved *for the use of the Methodist Society in Sheffield.* Vickers was a Methodist and the set possibly dates from very early in the 19th century.

Fig. 325 Communion set, c. 1825, including flagon, chalice, footed paten and christening basin.

Fig. 326 Large communion flagon by JAMES DIXON & SONS, 1835-1841. Mark No. 151.

194

Fig. 327 Pair of alms plates, 12¼ inches, by PHILIP ASHBERRY & SONS, 1856-1860. Mark No. 31.

Fig. 328 Communion plate or paten by PHILIP ASHBERRY & SONS, c. 1865. Mark No. 37.

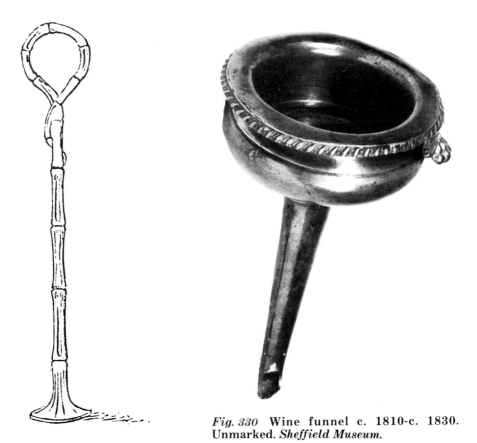

Fig. 329 Sugar crusher by BROADHEAD &
ATKIN. This design was registered May 19,
1848. Shown about actual size.

Fig. 330 Wine funnel c. 1810-c. 1830.
Unmarked. *Sheffield Museum.*

Fig. 331 Marrow scoop, c. 1820, unmarked.

Fig. 332 Rabbit pin cushion, c. 1870-1880. Unmarked.

Fig. 333 Pig match safe, the hinged head opens to reveal the matches, c. 1880. Unmarked.

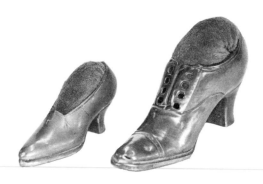

Fig. 334 A pair of swans, their use undetermined, but probably table salts, c. 1880. Unmarked.

Fig. 335 Pin cushion shoes-almost always made of lead with a very light coating of Britannia metal, c. 1870-c. 1900.

Fig. 336 A medal commemorating the opening of the University of Sheffield in July, 1905. The ceremony was attended by Edward VII.

Fig. 337 Loving or presentation cup, c. 1880. Unmarked. *Judith Marshall.*

Fig. 338 Fern pot by ATKIN BROTHERS, c. 1900. Mark No. 43.

Fig. 339 A pair of small vases marked PERIOD PEWTER, c. 1935-1940. Mark No. 111. *Boone's Antiques.*

Fig. 340 Potato pot by PHILIP ASH-BERRY, c. 1865. Mark No. 37.

*Fig. 341*Footed bowl by COOPER BROTHERS AND SONS, LTD., 1926-1939. Marks No. 114 and 115. *Boone's Antiques*

*Fig. 342*Footed bowl by COOPER BROTHERS & SONS, LTD., 1926-1939. Marks No. 114 and 115. *Boone's Antiques*

Fig. 343 Footed bowl marked CRAFTSMAN, by Viner's Ltd., c. 1935. Mark No. 474.

PEWTER FRUITS, BISCUITS, Etc.

760
Pewter Fruit Bowl, 8 in. dia.
Hand Chased, price £2 0 0

675
Pewter Cake or Fruit Dish.
9¾ in. dia. Hand Chased.
price £1 17 0

748
Pewter Cake or Fruit Stand.
9⅞ in. high, Hand Chased
price £2 13 0

602
Pewter Fruit or Rose Bowl.
Hand Chased, 8½ in. dia.
price £2 2 0

623
Pewter Casserole Stand, with
8 in. round "PYREX" Glass,
price £2 16 6

649
Pewter Sugar Dredger.
7 in. high, price £1 2 6

906
Pewter Cake or Fruit Basket,
9½ in. long, price £1 17 0

630
Pewter Sugar Dredger,
7 in. high, price £1 1 0

923
Pewter Tankard.
1 pint £1 2 6

800
Pewter Flower Vase,
7 in. high, price £1 2 6
8 in. ,, ,, £1 7 0

611
Pewter Tankard,
1 pint, price 19/6

752
Pewter Biscuit Box.
6½ in. high, price £1 10 0

928
Pewter Condiment Set, 3 piece £1 4 0
,, ,, Tray 6 0

862
Pewter Biscuit Box,
price £1 13 0

Fig. 344 **Hand hammered pewter table wares, c. 1935.**

JAMES
VICKERS
Who Departed this Life
April 1809

And finally, a coffin tag signifies an appropriate conclusion to this chapter of illustrations.

WARES KNOWN TO BE MADE IN SHEFFIELD
BUT NOT ILLUSTRATED

18th and 19th Centuries

Beakers
Caddy Spoons
Cruet Stands
Egg Cups
Knife Handles
Oil Bottles (gun oil)
Pap Boats
Spoon Warmers
Sugar Castors
Wine Coasters
Wine Coolers
Wine Lables

20th Century

Ash Trays
Biscuit, Butter, Cheese Stands
Bon Bon Dishes
Bread Knife Handles
Bread Platters
Butter Dishes
Cheese Box Holders
Cigarette Boxes
Desk Calendars
Glass Holders
Muffin Dishes
Sauce Bottle Holders

CHAPTER EIGHT
*The Makers
and Their Marks*

From the time when the first articles were made by James Vickers in 1769, nearly four hundred firms are known to have made white metal-Britania metal-pewter wares in Sheffield. The exact number is difficult to determine. It is academic whether to count a firm which was taken over by new owners and given a new name, as the same firm continuing under new management or to count them as two different firms having different names and management. Secondly, from about 1870, nearly all firms which engaged exclusively in the manufacture of electroplated goods used copper, Britannia metal or nickel silver as a base metal. How many, if any, of these firms produced unplated Britannia metal on occasion is unknown. It may be logically assumed, however, that Britannia metal wares produced by the electroplaters would have been limited. Of course many firms produced both electroplated and unplated wares and these firms are included in the list of makers.

The marks given in this chapter are those taken from existing examples. The absence of a mark next to a makers name in the list only indicates that a mark for that maker has not been recorded. It was the practice of all Sheffield makers to mark their goods and the absence of a mark should not be interpreted to mean that the maker produced unmarked goods. A full explanation of all marks is given in Chapter VI.

The working dates for each mark have been painstakenly researched, using many cross references which were then matched with known examples. The specific dates are certain. In the instances where the exact dates could not be determined, circa dated are used. In nearly all instances the circa dates are believed to be within two years of the actual date. When only one date is given, it means that the maker only worked that one year. Two plus marks beside a date indicates that the firm was still in existence at the time of publication.

Street addresses and their dates are given in the biographical sketches, for some makers included their address as part of their mark. This is often helpful in arriving at a specific manufacturing period.

In listing the makers by name, a slight break in alphabetical tradition has been made. Firms of a family origin and name are listed in chronological sequence rather then strict first name alphabetical order. This allows the reader to ascertain at a glance the history of a firm in the proper order of development.

Not all firms of the same surname are related. Relationships can be determined by date sequence.

The marks have been reproduced at actual size. Imperfections in lettering etc., may occasionally be evident. These are not the result of careless art work, but are exact reproductions of marks seen on actual wares. However, over a period of years makers used different punches, and variations in the marks, including overall size, do exist.

All of the makers listed worked in Sheffield with a few noted exceptions.

For convenience the author has added reference numbers to the makers and their marks.

Column 1. gives the surname for quick reference.

Column 2. lists the complete firm name(s) as well as working dates for various addresses, name changes and other information of interest.

Column 3. illustrates the known marks.

Column 4. dates the marks illustrated in column 3.

Column 5. identifies each maker or mark by a reference number.

SURNAME	Full name, adresses, working dates and biographical information.	Known marks	Dates	Ref. No.

1	2	3	4	5
	-A-			
ABBEY	See Osborne & Co.			
ABPC	The Association of British Pewter Craftsmen was organized in 1970 with the support of the Worshipful Company of Pewterers and oversees all aspects of design and manufacturing in modern pewter. Only members of the Association are permitted the use of Association touch marks which guarantee that the items marked have met stringent standards of metal content, gauge, finish, design and carftsmanship. Mark No. 1 first came into use in 1970 and Mark No. 2 dates from 1980.		1970++ 1980++	1 2
ADAM	Joseph Adam, c. 1821-c.1830. Adam was a spoon maker in the Attercliffe section of Sheffield. Evidence indicates that his work may have been limited to spoons made of iron.			3
ALLAN	James Allan worked from 1849 to 1872. His address was Wicker St. from 1869 to 1851, and Andrew St. from 1851 to 1855. In 1855 the "& Co." was dropped from the name and the firm moved to Johnson Lane where it remained until it closed in 1872. This firm should not be confused with James Allen & Co. which manufactured silver and plated wares from 1889 to 1960 under the trade names of Allen & Darwin, James Allen & Co. and Allen's. Note the different spelling of Allen.	J. ALLAN & CO SHEFFIELD JAMES ALLAN SHEFFIELD	1849-1855 1855-1872	4 5
ALLCARD	Allcard & Co., Albert Works, Norfolk St. This firm was listed with Arthur Culf & Co. as a joint company during the years 1895-1901.			6
ALLISON	Allison & Lonsdale, 137 Portobello Rd., 1884.			7
ANDERTON	Charles Anderton, 30 Townhead St., 1861-1886.			8

1	2	3	4	5
ARDRON	S. Ardron & Son, 12 Holly St., 1849-1858. Wares by Ardron are known but the marks are unrecorded. The firm was succeeded by A. E. Furniss in 1859.			9
ARMITAGES	Armitages & Standish, Eyre Ln., c.1829. This partnership is listed in error as an American firm by several authorities on American pewter. The firm is clearly indentified in the directories and rate books for Sheffield.	ARMITAGES & STANDISH	c.1829	10
ARUNDEL	Arundel Stainless Wares, Ltd., 67 Earl St., produced pewter wares from 1961 when they purchased the pewter department from Walker & Hall as that firm became part of British Silverware Ltd. One of the main shareholders in Arundel Stainless Wares was Pinder Brothers of Sheffield, whose financial interest increased until complete control was gained in 1977. The "Keep" mark was registered and first used in 1966 and ceased being used in March of 1977. Rights to future use of the mark are held by Pinder Brothers.	ENGLISH PEWTER MADE IN SHEFFIELD ENGLAND A.S.W	1961-1966	11
		Keep ENGLISH PEWTER MADE IN SHEFFIELD ENGLAND A.S.W.	1966-1977	12
ASHBERRY	John Ashberry & Sons was a 19th Century retail firm. Their name was stamped on goods made especially for them.	JOHN. A. ASHBERRY & SONS SHEFFIELD	c.1850-c.1860	13
	Philip Ashberry began as a spoon maker in 1829 at 15 Copper St. In 1839 a larger works was established at 21 Bowling Green St. where it remained until it closed in 1935. Ashberry developed one of the largest Britannia metal and subsequent electroplate manufactures in 19th century England. From about 1845 a complete range of goods were made with spoons and ladles always an important product. In 1856 "& Sons" was added to the name and marks. Ashberry became a limited company in 1900 and discontinued production under original family control in 1935 after 106 years of existence. Mark No. 14 was only used during 1829 and six months of the following year	ASHBERRY PATENT	1829-1830	14
		ASHBERRY PATENT	1830-1836	15
		BEST METAL ASH BER RY	1830-1836	16
		ASHBERRY BEST METAL	1830-1836	
		ASHBERRY BEST METAL WARRANTED FOR USE	1830-1836	18

210

1	2	3	4	5
	as the reign of George IV ended in 1930. Marks No. 15-20 were used on spoons and ladles made during the reign of William IV. Although marks No. 19 and No. 20 do not include the monarch's initial, note that the others include the WR. Spoons and ladles made during the reign of Queen Victoria received marks No. 21-25, which include the VR. Note that the old English style V on marks No. 21, 22 and 23 might easily be confused with the earlier W. Marks 26-28 were used on goods other than spoons and ladles from about 1845. Mark No. 28 appeared in 1856 and was also used later on 20th century pewter (see mark No. 41). Mark No. 29 was first used in 1856, the "& S" signifying the entry of the sons into partnership. About mid-19th century many makers including Ashberry, occasionally placed a steel wire in the shanks of their spoons to give them strength and reduce the tendency to bend. Mark No. 30 reflects the use of steel wire in spoons by Ashberry. Mark No. 31 was the standard mark before the introduction of the female figure Britannia which appeared in 1861. Mark No. 32 was used by many makers who used Samuel Russell's patented method for attaching handles to teapots to reduce heat in the handle. Marks No. 33 and 34 were used on early electroplated wares. Marks No. 35 and 36 were found on brass disks placed on the inside of teapot lids, where they acted as a reinforcement for strength under the knob. The registration date on No. 36 refers to registration of the female figure Britannia as Ashberry's mark. Mark No. 37, the figure of Britannia, adopted in 1861, is the most frequently seen mark on Ashberry goods other than spoons and ladles. Marks No. 38, 39 and 40 were used only on electroplated wares. In August, 1889, Ashberry received patent number 13,360 for his design of concentric lines on	BEST METAL FOR USE / ASHBERRY	1830-1836	19
		BEST METAL FOR USE / ASHBERRYS	1830-1836	20
		WR BEST METAL ASH BER RY	1837-c.1845	21
		WR BEST METAL WARRANTED FOR USE ASH BER RY	1837-c.1860	22
		WR ASHBERRY BEST METAL WARRANTED FOR USE	1837-c.1860	23
		VR BEST METAL WARRANTED FOR USE ASH BER RY	1837-c.1860	24
		VR ASHBERRY BEST METAL WARRANTED FOR USE	1837-c.1860	25
		PHILIP ASHBERRY	c.1845-1855	26
		PHILIP ASHBERRY SHEFFIELD	c.1845-1855	27
		PHILIP ASHBERRY & SONS	1856-c.1860	28
		P A & S	1856-c.1860	29
		PHILIP ASHBERRY & SONS PATENT STEEL WIRED	1856-c.1860	30
		PHILIP ASHBERRY & SONS SHEFFIELD	1856-c.1860	31

1	2	3	4	5
ASHBERRY (Cont')	the bottoms of teapots to allow movement of the bottom caused by heat. These teapots with corrugated bottoms are marked EXPANSION BOTTOM. Mark No. 41 was used on 20th century pewter wares. Note that the firm name appears as it did on mark No. 28, with the additional reference to pewter and England. In 1935 the remaining members of the Ashberry family closed the plant. Lewis Rose & Co., Ltd. purchased the site and demolished the old factory. The stock and goodwill were purchased by Mr. Stephenson who continued the electroplate trade under the Ashberry name on Eyre St. After World War II, Lewis Rose & Co., Ltd. bought the stock, Ashberry name and goodwill and moved back to Bowling Green St. In 1969 the firm was purchased by Spear & Jackson and in 1976 that firm was purchased by Guy Degrenne of France. At present the firm is known as Ashberry & Degrenne Ltd., Prospect Rd., Sheffield.	PATENT NONCONDUCTING HANDLE	1856-c.1875	32
		PA&S	1856-c.1890	33
		PA&S	1856-c.1890	34
		PHILIP ASHBERRY & SONS SHEFFIELD	1860-c.1890	35
		PHILIP ASHBERRY & SONS REGISTERED MAY. 18 1861 SHEFFIELD	1861-c.1890	36
		BRITANNIA PHILIP ASHBERRY & SONS SHEFFIELD	1861-c.1914	37
		PA&S	1867-1935	38
		ASHBERRY EP	1867-1935	39
		PA &SGP	c.1880-1935	40
		PHILIP ASHBERRY & SONS BEST ENGLISH PEWTER MADE IN ENGLAND	c.1920-c.1935	41
ASHFORTH	Joseph Ashforth worked from 1862 to 1871 at the following three addresses: 18 School Croft (1862-1863) 70 Snig Hill (1864-1870) 16 Love Street (1871)			42

212

1	2	3	4	5
ATKIN	Atkin Brothers of Truro Works, 169 Matilda St. en joyed a long history of manu facturing in Sheffield, which under their own name lasted from 1853 until 1964. The name of Atkin appears in the roster of craftsmen in the 18th century. In 1834 Henry Atkin formed a partnership with Rogers Broadhead. The firm of Broadhead and Atkin lasted until mid 1853 when two separ- ate companies were formed; R. Broadhead & Co. and Atkin Brothers, both of which survived into the 20th century. Atkin Brothers produced great quan- tities of silver and plated goods as well as Britannia metal. Also see Broadhead & Atkin; Holdsworth & Atkin.	ATKIN BROTHERS SHEFFIELD ATKIN BROTHERS SHEFFIELD MADE IN ENGLAND ESTD 1750 ATKIN BROTHERS SHEFFIELD MADE IN ENGLAND	1853-c.1909 c.1910-1947 c.1947-1964	43 44 45
	-B-			
BAILEY	Widow Bailey, a spoon maker worked at Smith St. From 1813-c.1815. It would be normal to assume that she succeeded to the business upon the death of her busband but incomplete records preclude any confirmation.			46
BAINES	Baines & Roberts. Henry Baines and William Roberts worked together at Shoreham St. for one year in 1856.			47
BARNASCONE	Henry Barnascone was born in Switzerland in 1825 and moved in Sheffield as a young man to work with his brother, Lewis, in the retail trade. Henry established his own business in 1868 selling Shef- field and Birmingham wares. Barnascone was not a maker, but quality goods made for him have been recorded with his name. These goods were made in the styles of 1845-1883. The firm became H. Barnas- cone & Son in 1884, and the firm became a limited company in 1909, ceasing operations in 1934.	H.BARNASCONE SHEFFIELD	c.1868-c.1883	48
BATEMAN	Ralph Bateman & Joseph Crookes, Bridge St. 1868.			49

1	2	3	4	5
BATT	John Batt began in the electro plate trade with his father, William Batt, in 1864. By 1868 he had established his own electroplate business. Batt is listed in the directories as a maker of Britannia metal for the years 1890-1920 and in keeping with other Sheffield firms produced the wares after World War I as "Best English Pewter". The trade mark PARK was used by Batt.	**J B & Co Lto** BEST ENGLISH PEWTER	1920-1938	50
BAUM	Maurice Baum worked from 1889 to 1903 at 191 Norfolk St. Baum was primarily a maker of electroplated goods and his trade mark, Silverine, registered in 1891, was used for electroplated goods.	SILVERINE	1891-1903	51
BAXTER	John Baxter, Bridgehouses, was listed in the 1787 directory as a maker of knives framed in white metal.	24 N	c.1787	52
BEARDSHAW	A. Beardshaw & Co. of Victoria St. was an electroplating firm dating from 1864-1924. Listings of 1889-1891 include Britannia metal goods.			53
BEATTIE	Richard Beattie & Co. of 37 Walker St. made spoons c. 1841			54
BEAUMONT	W. H. & J. Beaumont were three brothers, William, Henry and Joseph. The directories list this firm alternately as W. H. & J. Beaumont and as Beaumont Brothers. The firm existed from 1863 until 1917. Their addresses were Nursery Lane from 1863-1864, and Joiner Lane from 1865 to 1875, Corporation St. from 1876 to 1878, and Joiner Lane again from 1879 to 1917.			55
BELK	See Roberts & Belk.			
BETTS	Thomas Betts was listed among the electroplaters from 1919-1971, and also under the listings for pewter for 1948-1971. His address was 212 Brookhill and Sarah Lane, 1919-1964, and River Lane from 1965-1971. See also Furniss & Betts.			56

1	2	3	4	5
BIGGIN	Henry Biggin & Co., Arundel St., 1880-1884. Henry Biggin began in partnership with Wolstenholme in 1876, forming his own company in 1880. Also see Wolstenholme & Biggin.	HENRY BIGGIN & CO. SHEFFIELD	1880-1884	57
BINNEY	Joseph Binney, Broad Lane, was a maker of white metal framed knives. c.1785-c.1800.	THAT	c.1785-c.1800	58
BIRKS	William Birks was a spoon maker at 50 West St. 1841-1844.			59
BISHOP	William Bishop worked for three years under the following names: William A. Bishop, Nursery Lane, 1898-1899; William A. Bishop & Co., Surrey Lane, 1900-1909. A listing of 1900 also gives W. Bishop & Sons of Stanley St.			60
BLYDE	Edwin Blyde of 59 Eyre St., 1871.			61
	Edwin Blyde & Co., Charles Lane, 1872.			61
BOARDMAN	Boardman, Glossop & Co., Ltd., 171 Pond St., 1847-1927. Although an electroplate manufacturer, the firm is included with the Britannia metal makers for the years 1900-1903.			63
BOOTH	T. Booth was not a Sheffield maker but worked in Hanley, Staffordshire making Britannia metal lids for earthenware and porcelain jugs, c. 1840-c. 1870. Other marks were used.	T. BOOTH HANLEY	c.1840-c.1860	64
BOWER	Jospeh Henry Bower of Back fields worked from 1898 to 1920. In 1902 his address changed to 12 Arundel Lane; in 1911 the address changed to 28 Eyre Lane and in 1912 the name became Jospeh Henry Bower & Co.			65
BRADFORD	The *Sheffield Courant* of Sept. 14, 1793, announced the bankruptcy of Samuel Bradford, "white metal manufacturer".			66

1	2	3	4	5
BRADSHAW	William Bradshaw was a spoon maker at 9 Walker St., Wicker, from 1828 to 1830.			67
BRAMWELL	Bramwell, Brownhill & Co., Cyprus Works, Fawcett St., 1891-1894. Bramwell & Co., Cyprus Works, Fawcett St., 1895-1926. This firm succeeded Alfred Ecroyd and assumed Ecroyd's trade mark in 1891. Ecroyd had previously succeeded the Sheffield Plate Co. who originated the trade mark in 1884. The mark used by Bramwell was revised, leaving out the wheat sheaves and arrows originally included by the previous owners. The shield here was used during the entire existence of the firm, 1891-1939. However, additional marks such as, BEST ENGLISH PEWTER and HAND HAMMERED PEWTER, date 1920-1939. Also see Turner & Bramwell	RELIABLE (shield)	1891-1939	68
BRANSON	John Hugh Branson, 17 Syca more, 1859-1860. Branson began in partnership as Skinner, Coulson & Branson in 1854 Also see Skinner, Coulson & Branson; Skinner & Branson			69
BRAY	See Davenport & Bray			
BRENNAN	See Fisher & Brennan.			
BRIDDON	Briddon Brothers & Co., Enterprise Works, St. Mary's Road, 1908-1909.			70
BRIGGS	William Briggs, 1928-1862. His address from 1828 to 1840 was Carver Lane. From 1841-1862 the address was 38 Furnival St. In 1862-1864 a partnership was formed as Roberts & Briggs. In 1865 the firm became Roberts & Belk which continued in the electroplate trade into the 20th century.			71
	Briggs & Smith, Carver Lane, 1830. This was a short term, one year partnership of William Briggs (above) and Smith.			72

1	2	3	4	5
BRIGGS (Cont')	W. Briggs & Co., Johnson Lane, Andrew St. was formed in 1876 and lasted until 1922. This firm became a limited company and from 1901 became known as William Briggs & Co., Ltd., 1901-1922. Also see Roberts & Briggs.	WM. BRIGGS & CO. SHEFFIELD	1876-1900	73
BRIGHT	K. Bright Ltd., 112 Carver St., 1951-1959.	K. Bright Pewterer MADE IN SHEFFIELD ENGLAND	1951-1959	74
BROADBENT	J.W. Broadbent, Howard St., 1814.			75
BROADHEAD	Broadhead, Gurney, Sporle & Co., 17 Workhouse Croft, 1792-1800. This firm engaged in the manufacture of Sheffield Plate as well as Britannia metal. Although the firm under this organization was short lived, the Broadhead name remained in the trade until the year 1900. James Dixon served his apprenticeship with the senior partner, Samuel Broadhead.			76
	Samuel Broadhead worked from c. 1800-1829. His addresses were Angel St. from c. 1800-1820, and Queen St. from 1821-1829.			77
	R. (Rogers) Broadhead, Queen St., 1830-1833. The mark of R. Broadhead should not be confused with later marks No. 90, 91 and 92, of R. Broadhead & Co., which always included "& Co.".	R·BROADHEAD	1830-1833	78
	Broadhead & Atkin, 1834-1853. A great amount of quality wares were produced during this company's twenty years of existance. They were at North St. from 1834-1843 and during this period their mark included their North St. address. Additionally, the marks often included the capacity written out in half pints and/or indentification of features, such as: anti caloric handles or silver filbert knobs. Upon the move to Love St., mid-1843, the mark was simplified. Mark No. 85 is an oddity, however. The basic mark for William IV would date 1830-1836. It is probable	BROADHEAD & ATKIN NORTH STREET WORKS SHEFFIELD SILVER FILBERT KNOB	1834-1843	79
		V R BROADHEAD & ATKIN NORTH STREET WORKS SHEFFIELD SILVER FILBERT KNOB	1837-1843	80
		V R BROADHEAD & ATKIN NORTH STREET WORKS SHEFFIELD 5 HALF PINTS	1837-1843	81
		BROADHEAD & ATKIN NORTH STREET WORKS SHEFFIELD ANTI CALORIC HANDLE	1840-1843	82

1	2	3	4	5
BROADHEAD (Cont')	this this mark was used in early Victorian years under license from a patent granted by William IV. This mark is found on a coffee pot in the Sheffield Museum. During the period 1840-1850 many firms used the term *published by* for special items, especially those that were registered. Mark No. 87 is a unique mark used by Broadhead & Atkin during this period. Broadhead & Atkin introduced metal *anti caloric* handles to the industry (1840) and were one of the first to use filled silver knobs on tea and coffee pots. Mark No. 88 is found on earthenware jug lids. The jugs were purchased from Staffordshire and mounted with metal lids and subsequently sold by the Britannia metal firms. Electroplating began in 1843 and the Broadhead & Atkin mark No. 89 is one of the earliest known electroplate marks. In July of 1853 the partners split and two companies were formed, R. Broadhead & Co. and Atkin Brothers. Broadhead remained at the Love St. works while Atkin Brothers took over the Truro Works on Matilda St., previously owned by another Britannia metal firm, Joseph Cutts.	V ♛ R BROADHEAD & ATKIN NORTH STREET WORKS *SHEFFIELD* ANTI CALORIC HANDLE	1840-1843	83
		V ♛ R BROADHEAD & ATKIN NORTH STREET WORKS *SHEFFIELD* ANTI CALORIC HANDLE 5 HALF PINTS	1840-1843	84
		W ♛ R **PATENT** **BROADHEAD** **& ATKIN** **SHEFFIELD**	c.1843	85
		BROADHEAD **& ATKIN** **SHEFFIELD**	1843-1853	86
		Published by *BROADHEAD & ATKIN*	c.1846	87
		BROADHEAD & ATKIN	1843-1853	88
		B&AS	1846-1853	89
	R. Broadhead & Co., Love St., 1853-R 1900. Upon the dissolution of the Broadhead & Atkin partnership in mid 1853, Atkin Brothers took new facilities at Matilda St., while R. Broadhead remained at the Love St., premises. R. Broadhead was a large company which produced a great amount of Britannia metal, British Plate, electroplate and silver goods. Note that about 1859 the mark was altered to omit the R.	*R.BROADHEAD & Co* SHEFFIELD	1853-c.1859	90
		R. BROADHEAD & CO.	1853-c.1859	91
		BROADHEAD & Co SHEFFIELD	c.1859-1900	92
BROOKS	See A. R. Wentworth			
BROOKSBANK	Abram Brooksbank & Co., Malinda St., 1884-1889.	ABRAM BROOKSBANK SHEFFIELD	1884-1889	93

1	2	3	4	5
BROWN	William Brown, 53 Bailey St. c. 1814-1828.			94
	Brown, Tyler & Brown, Nursery Lane, c. 1829-1832.			95
	Brown & Tyler, Andrew St., c. 1832-1836			96
	Joseph Brown, 1837-1867. From 1837 to 1848 his address was Local Terrace. From 1849 to 1867 the address was 229 Rockingham	J. BROWN SHEFFIELD	1837-1867	97
	Brown & Lee, 229 Rockingham, 1868-1870. Out of his short partnership came the beginning of various Lee companies that lasted well into the 20th century.			98
BROWNHILL	See Bramwell, Brownhill & Co.			
BRUMBY	Brumby & Middleton, 32 Lambert St., 1894-1899. In 1900 the firm changed products, producing cutlery, particularly fruit and dessert knives.	BRUMBY & MIDDLETON SHEFFIELD	1894-1899	99
BULLISS	John Bulliss, 56 Suffolk, 1854			100
BUXTON	Buxton & Russell, 5 Duke St., 1852-1860. Samuel Russell had his own business prior to this partnership with Buxton. When the two separated in 1860 each formed their own companies, Samuel Russell working on his own for the second time.	BUXTON & RUSSELLS SHEFFIELD EXTRA HARD	1852-1860	101
		BUXTON & RUSSELL	1852-1860	102
	Edwin James Buxton & Co., Duke Place, St. Mary's Road, 1860-1863.			103
	-C-			
CALVERT	See I. Walkland & Co.			
CAMEO	See E. H. Parkin & Co., Ltd.			
CARPENDALE	Carpendale & Middleton, 115 Scotland St., c. 1862, Mark No. was used on electroplated wares.	C & M	c.1862	104
CARR	George Carr, 23 Smithfield, c. 1830			105
CHAMPION	Thomas Champion & Son, 37 High St. An advertisement of 1828 describes Champion as the manufacturer of a wide			106

1	2	3	4	5
CHAMPION (Cont')	range of goods, including Britannia metal wares. No other source, however, indicates that any Britannia metal goods were made by this firm.			
CHARLESWORTH	George Charlesworth was a spoon maker from 1849-1865 at numerous addresses.			107
CHELTENHAM	See E. H. Parkin & Co., Ltd.			
CIVIC	See T. Land & Son.			
CLARKE	Joseph Clarke, c. 1815-1823. His address was North St., c. 1815-1819 and 40 Lambert St. from 1820-1823.			108
	Jn (John) Clarke & Sons, 52 to 56 Harvest Lane, 1895-1921. (John Clarke and Son, Ltd., from 1906 to 1921.) This firm primarily produced electro-plated wares. Their marks are often seen however, on patent-ed, removable Britannia metal lids for jugs.	CLARKE'S PATENT	1895-1921	109
		J.C. & SONS	1895-1921	110
COBB	Frank Cobb & Co., 35 and 37 Howard St., 1903++. The Cobb Company primarily manufac-tured silverwares but pro-duced pewter wares under the trade description of Period Pewter from c. 1926 to 1939.	PERIOD PEWTER	1926-1939	111
COLDWELL	See Froggatt, Coldwell & Lean.			
CONSTANTINE	Richard Constantine, 1792-1830. James Dixon worked in the employ of Constantine for seven or eight years as a jour-neyman, before establishing his own business about 1804. Constantine's addresses were: Pea Croft, 1792-1800; Scotland St., 1800-1829 and Upper Thorp, 1830.	RICHARD CONSTANTINE	1792-1830	112
COOK	James Cook, 22 Suffolk Road, 1871.			113
COOPER	Cooper Brothers, Don Plate Works, began on High St. in 1866, moved to Bridge St. in 1872 and Arundel St. in 1886, and became Cooper Brothers & Sons Ltd., in 1895. The firm began with the manufacture of silver goods, and wares of that class have continued to be their main product. Britannia metal wares were listed from 1884 to 1908, and pewter wares produced from 1926 to the present. Cooper Brothers	C BROS S	1894++	114
		DON PEWTER	1926++	115
			1948-1969	116
			1969++	117

1	2	3	4	5
COOPER (Cont')	continues to be a leading Sheffield firm in the production of quality silver, electroplate and pewter wares. Mark No. 114 is the basic mark used on various wares from 1894. Mark No. 115 has been in use since the introduction of Don Pewter in 1926. The figure of a cooper represented in mark No. 116 also has been used on various wares but was used on pewter wares from 1948 to 1969. Mark No. 117 is an updated version of the "cooper", dating from 1969. Also see Marshall, Cooper & Co.			
CORNISH	See James Dixon & Sons			
COULSON	See Skinner, Coulson & Branson			
COUSINS	Joseph Cousins, 11 Garden St., c. 1828-1830. Cousins began in the Sheffield Plate trade in 1822 as Cousins & Co. In 1825 the firm became Hobson & Cousins, adding Britannia metal wares to their production. By 1828 the name became Joseph Cousins. Also see Hobson & Cousins			118
COWLISHAW	Henry Cowlishaw was a spoon maker from 1841-1872. His addresses were: 73 Broad St., 1841-c. 1855; Castle St., c. 1856-1859; 6 Wicker Lane, 1860-1871 and Stanley St. in 1872. During the latter years, Cowlishaw may have produced some other wares in addition to spoons.			119
CRAFTSMAN	See Viners Ltd.			
CROOKES	See Ralph Bateman & Joseph Crookes.			
CULF	Arthur Culf worked from 1872 to 1891 under the following names and addresses: Arthur Culf, 92 Wellington St., 1872-1875; Rock Works, 34 Charlotte St., 1876-1886; Arthur Culf & Co., Rock Works, 34 Charlotte St., 1887-1894; Allcard & Co. and Arthur Culf, Albert Works, Norfolk St., 1895-1901.			120

1	2	3	4	5
CULF (Cont')	Culf & Kay, 60 Wellington St., 1922++		1936-1960	121
	The firm of Culf & Kay was founded in 1922 with sporting gun cleaning implements as their main product along with spirit and hunting flasks. In 1936, the products changed to supply parts to the electroplate trade. One of the founders, Mr. Kay, died in the late 1930's and the co-founder, Mr. Culf, died during the war years. A.C. Culf, son of the founder, re-established the business in 1946 as a pewter manufactory, having purchased the electro-plate and pewter department from Harrison Fisher & Co., Ltd. The main products from 1946 have been pewter wares although electroplated silver goods are also produced. The Culfonia mark dates from 1946 and represents the house of Culf.	CULFONIA ENGLISH PEWTER	1946-1960	122
		CULF & KAY SHEFFIELD, ENGLAND	1946++	123
		Culfonia PEWTER	1960++	124
		Culfonia ENGLISH PEWTER	1960++	125
CUTTS	Joseph Cutts, spoon maker, 25 Hermitage St., c. 1841- c. 1847, 169 Matilda St., c. 1848- c. 1853. Tea wares were added in the latter years. In 1853 the premises were taken over by Atkin Brothers.	BEST METAL WARRANTED FOR USE J CUTTS	c.1841-c.1853	126
	Charles Cutts, Howard Lane, 1854, St. Phillips, c. 1856, spoon maker.			127
	Cutts Brothers, 1854-1863. From 1854 to 1855 the address was St. Mary's Road. From 1856 to 1863 the address was Pond St.			128
	George Cutts, 1859-1882. The address was 26 Sheaf & 53 Arundel from 1859 to 1862. In 1862 Cutts took over the premises at Broad St. which had been vacated by the Wolstenholme firm.			129
	George Cutts & Sons, Park Works, Broad St., Park, 1883-1896.			130
	-D-			
DAVENPORT	Davenport & Bray, Albion Works, 57 Eyre St., 1871-c. 1874.			131

1	2	3	4	5
DAVENPORT (Cont')	George Davenport, 57 Eyre St., c. 1875-1884			132
DAWSON	Dawson & Pallett, 68 Countess Road, 1923-1924.			133
DEAKIN	Although the Deakin family name does not appear in the Britannia metal trade until 1841, the family had been involved in Sheffield trades for many years prior to that date. John Deakin of Spring St. was a fork maker in 1797 and the family remained in the cutlery trade until 1841.			
	Joseph Deakin, Spring St., 1841-1852. Joseph Deakin (Jr.) produced spoons only for the first eight years, expanding to other goods about 1849.			134
	Deakin & Staniforth, Green Lane, 1853-1855.			135
	Joseph Deakin & Sons, Green Lane, 1856-1863, and Spring St. Works from 1864-1889. The corporate mark 3573 was first registered in 1856.	JOSEPH DEAKIN & SONS SHEFFIELD	1856-1864	136
		JOSEPH DEAKIN & SONS SPRING STREET WORKS SHEFFIELD	1864-1889	137
		JOSEPH DEAKIN & SONS SPRING STREET WORKS SHEFFIELD	1864-1889	138
	James Deakin & Co., 97 Matilda St. c. 1868-1870.			139
	James Deakin & Sons, Matilda St., 1871-1936. From 1901 to 1936 manufacture was limited to silver and electroplated wares. Mark No. 141 shows the James Deakin trade mark (enlarged). The mark dates from 1871, and was used primarily for electroplated wares. Marks No. 142 and 143 shows the use of the trade mark incorporated with marks used on dram flasks, many of which were unplated. Several variations were used.	JAMES DEAKIN & SONS SHEFFIELD	1871-c.1900	140
			1871-1936	141
		J. DEAKIN & SONS	1871-1936	142
		J D S	1871-1936	143
	G. Deakin & Co., 107 Edward St., 1901-1909. Manufacturer of electroplated wares.			144
DEWSNOP	See Hodgkinson, Dewsnop & Lowe.			

1	2	3	4	5
DIXON	The James Dixon firm has produced more Britannia metal/pewter wares than any other single company. Additionally, they have made quantities of Sheffield Plate, British Plate, electroplate, sterling silver and a wide variety of hunting assessories. In recent years they have been particularly known for their trophies made for major sports events. Until the death of Milo Dixon in 1976, the firm had remained under the control of direct surname descendants of the founder. Chapter III is devoted entirely to the history of the Dixon firm.	DIXON	1804-c.1810	145
		DIXON & SMITH	c.1811-1822	146
		DIXON & SON	1823-1829	147
			1824-1829	148
		JAMES DIXON & SON	1830-1834	149
	Mark No. 145 is given by Bradbury in *Old Sheffield Plate.* Evidence strongly suggests that Dixon worked alone from c. 1804 to 1810. If so, the use of the last name for the mark is characteristic. However, no examples with this are known. Mark No. 146 was used by the Dixon & Smith partnership at least from 1811 until 1822. Mark No. 147 is the basic mark from 1823-1829. Mark No. 148 is an escutcheon applied to Imperial standard measures. Mark No. 149 is the basic mark for the period 1830-1834 when "James" was added to the previous mark. Mark No. 150 is a rare mark found on a pair of spoons. The initials are those of William IV (1830-1836). The trumpet and banner device was later registered by Dixon in 1879. The registered mark would seem then to have been a revival of the rare and limited earlier use during the reign of William IV. Mark No. 151 is the basic mark for 1835-c. 1841, adding the S to Son of the earlier mark. Mark No. 152 is of the same period, omitting the James for reasons of space on small items such as lids for jugs and ladles. It has been known on teapots, however. Marks No. 153, 154, and 155 (intaglio) were used on smaller items such as flasks and boxes. During the period c. 1829-1842, the pattern number included with the mark on tea		1830-1834	150
		JAMES DIXON & SONS	1835-c.1841	151
		DIXON & SONS	1835-c.1841	152
		JAMES DIXON & SONS	1835-c.1841	153
		JAMES DIXON & SONS	1835-c.1841	154
		JAMES DIXON & SONS	c.1842 c.1851	155
		Published by Jas Dixon & Sons Sheffield March 1st 1842	1842	156
		JAMES DIXON & SONS	c.1842-c.1851	157

1	2	3	4	5
DIXON (Cont')	wares was occasionally accompanied by the letter C. Evidence tends to indicate that the letter C was used to identify tea services exported to America. Mark No. 156 was used on a colorful earthenware lidded jug, which was the first ceramic object registered under the design registration act of 1842. Similar marks were used for other special designs, most of which were registered between the years 1842-1846. Mark No. 157 is the basic mark for c. 1842-c. 1851. Mark No. 158 includes Best Britannia Metal, which refers not to the quality of the alloy, but to the overall quality of construction and component parts. Mark No. 159 is a special intaglio mark used on coffee pots and teapots registered in 1850. Mark No. 160 was used primarily on the lids of earthenware jugs where space was limited. Mark No. 161 is the basic mark for c. 1851-1879. Mark No. 162 was used on powder flasks. Note the inclusion of Sheffield. Mark No. 163 was used occasionally on glass bottomed tankards, where space was limited. Mark No. 164 is the basic mark from 1879++ when the trumpet and banner was registered as a trade mark. Mark No. 165 used on unique patented self pouring teapots. Mark No. 166 dates from the introduction of the trade description Cornish Pewter in 1927. Mark No. 167 dates from 1929, when the firm became a limted company and was used on a few special items.	JAMES DIXON & SONS BEST BRITANNIA METAL	c.1842-c.1851	158
			1850	159
		JAMES DIXON	c.1841-c.1851	160
		JAMES DIXON & SONS SHEFFIELD	c.1851-1879	161
		JAMES DIXON & SONS SHEFFIELD	c.1851-c.1870	162
		JAMES DIXON & SONS	c.1860-1879	163
		JAMES DIXON & SONS SHEFFIELD	1879-1927	164
		ROYLES PATENT SELF POURING Nº 6327 1886 MANUFACTURED BY JAMES DIXON & SONS SHEFFIELD FOR J.J. ROYLE MANCHESTER	1886-c.1895	165
		JAMES DIXON & SONS SHEFFIELD Cornish Pewter	1927++	166
		J. DIXON & SONS Lᵗᵈ SHEFFIELD	1929++	167

1	2	3	4	5
DIXON (Cont')	John Dixon & Co., 145 Allen St., c. 1848-1849.			168
	John Dixon & Sons, 40 Smithfield St., 1850-1852. The John Dixon firm was unrelated to James Dixon & Sons.			169
DON	See Cooper Brothers			
DORE'	See Roberts & Dore'.			
	-E-			
EALES	See PMC.			
EATON	William C. Eaton, 1883-1908. Located at Sidney St., 1883-1887 and 55 Howard St., 1888-1908.			170
	John Eaton, 53 Snig Hill, 1893-1896.			171
	T. W. Eaton & Co., Albert Works, 1899-1910. Located at Albert Works, 28 Cambridge St., 1899-1903, and Solly St., 1904-1910. Primarily electroplated goods.	V ♛ R T.W. EATON & CO. SHEFFIELD	1899-1901	172
		T.W. EATON & CO. SHEFFIELD	1902-1910	173
ECROYD	Alfred R. Ecroyd, Cyprus Works, Fawcett St., 1884-1890. Ecroyd succeeded the short lived Sheffield Plate Co., who originated the *Reliable* trade mark in 1884. Ecroyd was succeeded by Bramwell, Brownhill & Co. in 1891 (q.v.) who continued a revised version of the trade mark.		1884-1890	174
	-F-			
FALDING	See Hattersley & Falding.			
FATTORINI	Fattorini was not a maker, but a retailer with outlets in various towns in the north of England. Known examples have been of the 1870-1900 period. The firm continues at present as a retail jeweler.			175
FEARNLEY	Linder Fearnley, 58 Bridge St., 1851-1852.	LINDER FEARNLEY SHEFFIELD	1851-1852	176
FENTON	Fenton Brothers primarily produced electroplated wares from 1859-1919. the firm was listed as a Britannia metal manufacturer in 1889.			177

1	2	3	4	5
FIRTH	Firth & Holmes, 3 Burgess St., c. 1849.			178
FISHER	Harrison Fisher, Trafalgar St., 1898-1901. Harrison Fisher & Co., Wellington St. and Trafalgar St., 1902-1965. Although primarily an electroplate maker, Fisher produced wares under the trade name of Trafalgar.		1898-1939	179
	Fisher & Brennan, 23 & 25 Paternaster Row, 1865-1868.			180
	Also see Shaw & Fisher.			
FLANAGAN	Flanagan & Paramore, May's Yard, 52 Pond St., 1865.			181
FOWLER	F. J. Fowler worked from 1833-1860 at the following addresses: New Church, 1833-1844 26 Andrew, 1845-1848 17 Copper, 1849-1853 Suffolk St., 1854-1855 120 Harvest Lane, 1856-1857 Copper St., 1858-1860	F.J.FOWLER SHEFFIELD	1833-1860	182
FROGGATT	Froggatt, Coldwell & Lean, Eyre St., 1792-c. 1800.			183
	Henry Froggatt, Norfolk St., 1792-1795; Eyre St., 1796-1819.	FROGGATT	1792-1819	184
		FROGGATT	1792-1819	185
	Froggatt & Co., Eyre Lane (St.), 1820-1823.			186
	James & Charles Froggatt, 30 Eyre St., 1824-1826.			187
	James Froggatt, 30 Eyre St., 1827-1829.			188
	Froggatt & Owen, 33 Eyre St., 1830.			189
FURNISS	Arthur E. Furniss succeeded S. Ardron & Son and worked from 1859 to 1910. From c. 1900 wares were mostly electroplated goods. After 1910 the firm added "& Sons". Patents were granted in 1877 for ceramic (porcelain and earthenware) liners for teapots, coffee pots, jugs, etc. and removable strainers or grates. 12 Holly St., 1859-1862. 32 Rockingham, 1863-1870. 27 Carver St., 1871-1899. 62 Broad Lane and 13 Garden St., 1900-1910.	A.E.FURNISS SHEFFIELD ⬦Ⓐ⬦ A.E.FURNISS PATENT SHEFFIELD	1859-1910 c. 1870-1910 c. 1877-c. 1900	190 191 192

1	2	3	4	5
FURNISS (cont')	Arthur E. Furniss & Sons, 62 Broad Lane and 13 Garden St., 1911-1922. Primarily electroplated wares.			193
	Furniss & Betts, 51 Division St., 1911-1913. See Thomas Betts.			194
	James Furniss, Ltd., 1914++. This firm was an outgrowth of Furniss & Betts, established in 1911. At the outbreak of World War I, the partners formed separate companies which were, Thomas Betts (q.v.) and James Furniss Ltd. The company is a member of the Association of British Pewter Craftsmen and is unrelated to the earlier firm of A.E. Furniss & Sons. 51 Division St., 1914- 1924 4 Eyre Lane, 1925-1935 115 Portobello St., 1935-1945 16A Orange St., 1945++			195
GALLIMORE	-G- William Gallimore, 40 Lambert St., c. 1839.			196
	Eliz. Gallimore, 42 School Croft, c. 1859			197
	William Gallimore & Co., 17 Arundel, 1864-1887.			198
	John Gallimore, Italian Works, Matilda St., 1893-1914.			199
GIBSON	I. Gibson & Son, 113 Arundel, 1969-1971.			200
GLADWIN	Samuel Gladwin, Eyre Lane, 1912-1913.			201
	Gladwin Ltd., Embassy Works, Rockingham St., c. 1930			202
GLAVE	Joseph Glave, 1889-1910. 9 Charles Lane, 1889-1907. 3A Charles Lane, 1908. Wentworth Works, Burgess St., 1909-1910.			203
GLOSSOP	See Boardman, Glossop & Co., Ltd.			
GOODISON	William Goodison, 25 Monmouth St. and 100 Broomhall St., 1861-1884. Primarily a spoon maker.			204

1	2	3	4	5
GORDON	George Gordon & Son, 129 St. Mary's Road, 1913-1926. Succeeded by Gordon & Tyas.			205
	Gordon & Tyas, 188 Solly St., 1927-1953. Succeeded by F. A. Tyas (q.v.).			206
GOWER	An interesting obituary of 1813 gives Nathaniel Gower credit for being the father of the white metal trade. Gower was said to have entered the trade some 40 years earlier (1773) with a partner, Georgious Smith. His tenure in the trade was very short lived, as he gave up the partnership and entered the Sheffield Plate trade as a journey man. James Vickers has been confirmed as the founder of the industry which produced goods under the successive titles of *White Metal*, *Britannia Metal* and *Pewter*.			207
GRAMBLES	Samuel Grambles, 3 Union Lane, 1905.			208
GRAYSON	Benjamin Grayson & Son worked from 1871-1914. 19 Carver St., 1871-1875 Holly St., 1876-1886 18 Garden St., 1887-1899. 99 Napier St., 1900-1914.	B. GRAYSON & SON SHEFFIELD	1871-1914	209
GREAVES	John Greaves, Back Water Lane, c. 1841. Spoon maker.			210
GREEN	Green, Sampson & Green, Bridge St., 1821-1822.			211
	Green, Sampson & Co., Bridge St., 1823.			212
	Green & Marsh, Bridge St., 1824-1825.			213
	Also see Meeson & Green.			
	-H-			
HALE	Hale Brothers, 11 Allen St., 1884.			214
HALL	William Henry Hall, 111 Eldon St., 1908-1909.			215
	Hall Brothers, 32 Arundel St., 1951-1960; 61 Nursery, 1961-1971.			216

1	2	3	4	5
HALL (cont')	Hall & Phoenix, Smith's Works, Sidney St., 1891.			217
	Also see Martin, Hall & Co.; Walker & Hall.			
HANCOCK	Hancock & Jessop, Norfolk St., 1790-1794. This short lived partnership also produced Old Sheffield Plate.			218
	William Hancock, Upper St., Philips Rd., 1876-1884.			219
HARDY	Francis Hardy, 13 Devonshire Lane, 1895.			220
	Also see Ridge, Woodcock and Hardy; Woodcock and Hardy.			
HARPHAM	Brian Harpham, 32a Carver St., 1961.			221
HARRIS(S)	G. W. Harris(s) & Co., 57 Arundel, St., 1845-1863. From 1860 the address is given as 83 Arundel St. The partner in this company was Henry Land who began his own firm in 1864 with the advertisement "Late Harriss & Land".			222
	George Harriss, Burgess, 1859			223
	George Frank Harriss, Milton Works, 81 Milton St., and 148 Richard Rd., Heeley, 1881-1887. In 1887 the address is given as Jessop St.			224
HARRISON	John Harrison & Son, Hollis Croft, was listed in the 1787 directory as a maker of knives framed in white metal.	♱ ♡ I H	c. 1787	225
	J. (John) Harrison worked from 1833 to 1889 and was the first in Sheffield to electroplate goods (June 13, 1843). It was the 4th license granted by Elkingtons of Birmingham. By 1864 John Harrison had died, the firm being run by the executors. In 1884 the firm became "& Co." and Limited in 1886. Norfolk Lane, 1833-1843; 116 Scotland, 1844-1889.			226
	Henry Harrison & Co. Atwell Works, Pond Hill, 1876-1879.			227
	William W. (William Wheatcroft) Harrison & Co. was a major firm which produced the full line of electroplated	W.W.H. & CO.	1865-1911	228

1	2	3	4	5
HARRISON (cont')	goods. The working dates lasted from 1865-1911, being a Limited Company from 1909. Montgomery Works, 1865-1886; Rockingham St., 1887-1911.			
	Harrison Brothers, Tudor St., and Surry St., 1857-1861. Primarily electroplated wares.			229
	Harrison Brothers & Howson, 45 Norfolk, 1862-1899; Carver St., 1900-1909.			230
	Also see Petfield, Harrison & Wilson.			
HATTERSLEY	Hattersley & Falding, Snider Works, 105 Napier St., 1879-1887. From 1881, the Napier address is given as 109.			231
HAWKSLEY	The Hawksley firm produced copper powder flasks for hunters as well as dram or gin flasks of silver, electroplate and Britannia metal. Silver marks in the name of G. Hawksley & Co. were registered in 1856. The address was 32 Charlotte St., 1856, and Carver St. from 1865. The firm existed until 1946 when taken over by James Dixon & Sons.	G &J W HAWKSLEY	c. 1856-c. 1880	232
HAWKSWORTH	See Howard & Hawksworth.			
HEELEY	Heeley Brothers, Netherthorpe St., 1891-1892.			233
	Heeley & Burdekin, Netherthorpe St., 1893-1894.			234
	Heeley & Co., Neptune Works, Watery Lane, 1895-1901. (Assumed by John Nodder & Sons in 1899.)	WIGNALL HEELEY & CO. SHEFFIELD	1895-1901	235
HEPPENSTALL	John Heppenstall, Scotland St., c. 1828. Spoon maker.			236
HERALDIC	See John Round			
HERRIOTT	E. Herriott & Sons, 51 Backfields, 1902-1903.			237
HIBBERD	William Hibberd was a white metal founder in Sheffield in 1797.			238
	Frederick Hibberd, 23 Burgess St., 1871.			239

1	2	3	4	5
HIDES	Frank Hides, 57 Trafalgar St. and Devonshire Lane, 1881.			240
HILL	Thomas Hill, 47 Norfolk St., 1884.			241
HILTON	David Hilton, 66 Trinity, 1852-1855; 85 Edward St., 1856-1858; Upper St., 1859.			242
	David Hilton & Son, 56 St. Philips Rd., 1860-1861; 17 Orange St., 1862.			243
HL	Wares marked H L & Co. were made in Sheffield during the 1930's for Hamilton Laidlaw, wholesale jewelers in Glasgow, Scotland.	**H L & C** SHEFFIELD	c.1925-c. 1939	244
HOBSON	Samuel Hobson, Sheffield Moor, c. 1814. Button Maker.			245
	Hobson & Cousins, 2 Brocco St., 1824-1826.			246
HODGKINSON	Hodgkinson, Dewsnop & Lowe, Morpeth, 1841.			247
HOLDSWORTH	The Holdsworth tradition of spoon making touched three centuries in Sheffield. William Holdsworth began making white metal spoons at Water Lane in 1786. By 1809, William had died and the business was carried on by his widow, Martha. In mid-year, 1813, the business split, with the widow moving to Charles Street while the son, William, moved to Castle Street. About 1835 William the younger died and was succeeded by his widow, Sarah. A grandson to the founder, Henry Holdsworth, assumed the business in 1838 and was joined by his sons in 1864. The firm closed in 1900.			
	William Holdsworth, Water Lane, 1786-1813.	HOLDSWORTH	1786-1813	248
	Martha Holdsworth, 45 Charles St., 1813-1815.			249
	William Holdsworth Jr., Castle St., 1813-1828; 14 Angel St., 1829-1834.			250
	Sarah Holdsworth, 1 Queen St., 1835-1837.			251
	Henry Holdsworth, 1 Queen St., 1838-c. 1850; Arundel St., c. 1850-1863.		1838-1863	252

1	2	3	4	5
HOLDSWORTH (cont')	Henry Holdsworth & Sons, 83 Arundel St., 1864-1875; Bramall Lane, 1876-1900. The firm of Henry Holdsworth & Sons produced a full line of wares including electroplated goods, in addition to spoons.	HOLDSWORTH & SONS	1864-1900	253
	Holdsworth & Atkin, Whiteleywood Works, 1845. Spoon makers.			254
HOLMES	See Firth & Holmes.			
HOMELAND	See Walker & Co.			
HOMESTEAD	See Walker & Hall.			
HOWARD	Howard & Hawksworth, Orchard Lane, 1854-1856.			255
	E. Stirling Howard, Orchard Lane, 1857-c. 1862.			256
	E. Howard & Son, 90 Pond St. c. 1863-1864.			257
	Also see Walker & Hall.			
HOWE	Wm. Howe & Co., 17 Corporation St., 1859-1862.			258
				259
	Wm. Howe, Lambert St., 1862-1867; Woolen St., Infirmary Rd., 1868-1870; Robert St., Infirmary Rd., 1871-1879.			
	Mrs. Martha Howe, 48 Robert St., 1880-1881.			260
HOWSON	See Harrison Brothers & Howson.			
HOYLAND	John Hoyland, 13 Hawley Croft., 1868.			261
HUDSON	See Oates & Hudson.			
HUNTER	M. Hunter & Sons, Talbot Works, 328 Saville St., 1884 1887.	M. HUNTER & SONS TALBOT WORKS SHEFFIELD	1884-1887	262
HUTTON	Wm. Carr Hutton began in 1800 as a close plater of Old Sheffield Plate with primary wares of snuffers, spurs, tools, etc., made of steel and plated with silver. In 1843 Hutton received the second license in Sheffield to electroplate goods. They produced some Britannia metal wares under the name	Wm H&S IMPROVED METAL	1902-1930	263

1	2	3	4	5
HUTTON (cont')	of Wm. Hutton & Sons, from about 1860. The famed crossed arrows were taken over as a trade mark from the old firm of Creswick in 1902. The crossed arrows marks include both six and eight arrows. Hutton was taken over by James Dixon & Sons in 1930.	HUTTON SHEFFIELD	1902-1930	264
HYDES	Francis William Hydes, 74 Jericho St., 1876-1883; Leiscester St., 1884-1888; 78 Bowden St., 1889. Also see Sharman & Hydes. -I- No entries. -J-			265
JACKSON	Jackson & Walton, 1 Allen St., 1859; Scotland St., 1860-1864.			266
	F.E.T. Jackson & Co., 9 Eyre Lane, 1903-1904.			267
	Wilfred Jackson, 77 Hollis Croft, 1868-1891.			268
JERVIS	William Jervis, 1 White Croft, 1785-1800. White metal cutler.		1785-1800	269
	John Jervis, Meadow St., was a maker of knives framed in white metal, c. 1785-c. 1800.	C	1785-c. 1800	270
JESSOP	See Hancock & Jessop.			
JOHNSON	Christopher Johnson & Co., Portobello St., 1896++. Mainly electroplated wares, 1896-1940, and cutlery from 1940 to present.	C. JOHNSON & CO. SHEFFIELD	1896-c. 1939	271
		CHR'ST. JOHNSON & CO. SHEFFIELD	1896-c. 1939	272
	Also see Lucas & Johnson; Webster & Johnson's. -K-			
KAY	John Kay, Meadow St., c. 1828-1841. Spoon maker. Also see Culf & Kay.			273
KEEP	See Arundel Stainless Ware; Pinder Brothers.			
KENT	See PMC.			

1	2	3	4	5
KIRKBY	The Kirkby family was prominent in the 18th and early 19th century silver and Sheffield Plate trade. The short lived partnership of Kirkby, Smith & Co. produced wares about 1796-1797.			274
KITCHING	This family name was occasionally entered as Kitchens but marked goods bear the name Kitching.			
	(John) Kitching & Co., Church St., 1821; Norfolk Lane, 1822-1832; Green Lane, 1833-1827.			275
	Samuel Kitching (Kitchen), 5 Green Lane, 1830.			276
	George Kitching, Lambert Place, 1835-1845.	W ♔ R G.KITCHING PATENT	1835-1836	277
		V ♔ R G.KITCHING SHEFFIELD	1837-1845	278
	Also see Robinson & Kitching.			
	-L-			
LAND	Henry Land began in partnership with George Harriss as Harriss & Co. in 1845. In 1864 Land began his own business as electroplater to the trade. The firm went through several name changes to eventually become T. Land & Son, Ltd.			
	Henry Land, 23 Orchard Lane, 1864-c. 1874.	LAND	1864-c. 1874	279
	Thomas Land, 13 Cheney Row, c. 1875-1880; 56 Carver St., 1880-1889.			280
	George Land & Co., 15 West St., 1882-1885.			281
	Elizabeth Land, 23 Wellington St., 1886-1889.			282
	Land & Opley, 154 Fitzwilliam St., 1890-1892; Nimrod Works, 111 Eldon St., 1893-1897; 107 Trafalgar St., 1898-1901.			283
	T. Land & Son, 107 Trafalgar St., 1902-1905.			284

1	2	3	4	5
LAND (cont')	T. Land & Son, Ltd., Trafalgar St., 1906-1908; Queens Road, 1908-1952. In 1952 the firm was taken over by E. H.Parkin (q.v.) who continued the use of the CIVIC trade mark until 1977.	TRADE CIVIC MARK PEWTER	c. 1920-1939	285
		REGISTERED CIVIC TRADE MARK	1945-1977	286
LEE	The Lee firms had origins with William Brown, c. 1814 and the successive Brown firms (q.v.).			
	Lee & Wigfull, Charlotte St., 1871-1878; John St., 1879-1968.	G S L	1879-c. 1900	287
	James Lee & Co., 87 Eldon St., 1876-1885.	SUPERIOR BRITANNIAMETAL SHEFFIELD J. LEE&Co.	1876-1885	288
	Lee Brothers, 87 Eldon St., 1883.			289
	Lee, White & Co., 87 Eldon St., 1886-1887.	LEE & COMPY SHEFFIELD	1886-1887	290
	George Lee & Co., 87 Eldon St., 1888++. George Lee used the MY LADY trade mark from 1929. In 1967 the firm was taken over by Julius Isaacs & Co. Ltd., who continued the use of ARCADIA. The MY LADY mark was retained but received very limited use after 1967.	MY LADY ENGLISH PEWTER G. L & Cº.S	1929-c. 1967	291
		ARCADIA	c. 1950++	292
	Also see Brown & Lee; Reaney, Lee & Co.			
LEVICK	See Owen & Levick.			
LINDLEY	Alfred Lindley, Richmond Works, 168 Eldon St., 1883-1887; Richmond Works, Napier St., 1888-1889; 27 Eyre St., 1890-1896.			293
LODGE	James Lodge, 100 West St., 1901-1907; 70 Trafalgar St., 1908-c. 1919; 216 Solly St., 1920++. The James Lodge firm was founded in 1901 as an electroplate manufacturer. Pewter wares were added in the 1960's (to the trade only).			294

1	2	3	4	5
LONSDALE	See Allison & Lonsdale.			
LOWE	See Hodgkinson, Dewsnop & Lowe.			295
LUCAS	Lucas & Johnson, Shoreham St., 1871-1872.			
LUDLAM	Widow Ludlam and Sons, Burgess St., were makers of knives framed in white metal. c. 1785-c. 1800.	ETNA	c. 1785-c. 1800	296
	-M-			
MACLAURIN	J. Maclaurin & Son, 70 Bowden St., 1865-1872. The directories list this firm occasionally as "& Sons".			297
	Maclaurin Brothers, Sidney St., 1876-1893.			298
	George Maclaurin & Son, 117 Matilda St., 1883-1893.			299
	Herbert Maclaurin, Matilda St., 1894-1909.			300
	Also see Wolstenholme, Maclaurin, & Co.,			
MALLOY	Henry Malloy, Smith's Wheel, Sidney St., 1881-1883.			301
MANOR	See A. Milns.			
MANOR PERIOD	See Travis, Wilson & Co., Ltd.			
MARKHAM	Wallace Markham, 191½ Rockingham St., 1861-1863.			302
MARPLES	Charles Marples, 144 Eyre St., 1903-1908.			303
	Marples, Wingfield & Wilkins, Sykes Works, 148 Eyre St., 1909-1935; Portland Works, 75-77 Hill St., 1936-1953; 156a Fitzwilliam St., 1954.			304
MARSH	See Green & Marsh.			
MARSHALL	Marshall, Cooper & Co., Spring St., c. 1812-c. 1816.			305
	Marshall & Co., Carver Lane, c. 1817.			306
	Also See Parkin & Marshall.			

1	2	3	4	5
MARSHES	Marshes & Shepherd, c. 1825-c. 1845. This firm did not manufacture wares, but sold various Sheffield products stamped with their name.	MARSHES & SHEPHERD	c.1825-c. 1845	307
MARTIN	Frederick Martin, 199 Arundel St., 1887.			308
	Martin, Hall & Co., Broad St., Park, 1925-1929.			309
MATTHEWS	See Wardle & Matthews.			
MEESON	Meeson & Green, Orchard Works, Orchard Lane, 1876-1883.			310
	Meeson & Sons, Orchard Works, Orchard Ln. 1883-1888.			311
METHLEY	Methley & Wilson, 94 Wellington St., 1864.			312
MIDDLETON	See Carpendale & Middleton.			
MILLER	Miller & Wolstenholme, Spring St., 1821. This partnership was the beginning of the prominent firm of J. Wolstenhome (q.v.).			313
MILNS	A. Milns & Co., 89 Arundel St., 1906-1926. Milns manufactured electroplated wares but produced pewter wares under the trade description of Manor Pewter from c. 1920 to 1926. When the firm closed in 1926, the pewter business was assumed by Travis, Wilson & C., Ltd, who registered the trade name of Manor Pewter as part of their own new mark, 'Manor Period Pewter', in that year.	MANOR A M & Cᵒ M SHEFFIELD PEWTER	c. 1920-1926	314
MORTON	John Morton, 37 Furnace Hill, 1807-1817.			315
MOSS	Isaac Moss advertised in 1845 as being a manufacturer and dealer in all classes of Sheffield goods, including Britannia metal. It is doubtful, however, that any Britannia metal goods were made by Moss.			316
MY LADY	See George Lee & Co.			
	-N-			
NAYLOR	Naylor & Son, Coalpit Lane, were makers of knives framed in white metal. c. 1785-c. 1800.	PRET	c.1785-c. 1800	317

1	2	3	4	5
NEILL	Jas. Neill, Globe Works, Penistone Road, 1889.			318
NICHOLSON	Nicholson & White, North St., 1855. A short partnership with John White (q.v.).			319
NODDER	John Nodder & Sons, 1863-1902. The firm became a limited company in 1898 and assumed Heeley & Co. (q.v.) in 1899. 188 Rockingham, 1863-1864; Taranaki Works, 1865-1867; Taranaki Works, Dunfields, 1868-1875; Taranaki Works, Edward St., 1876-1888; 226 Brook Hill, 1889-1902.	JOHN NODDER & SONS SHEFFIELD	1863-1902	320
NOELLE	Noelle Brothers, 121 Rockingham St., 1890.			321
NOWILL	John Nowill & Sons, 135 Scotland St., 1884-1889. Nowill has origins as early as 1867 in the cutlery trade but does not appear among the Britannia metal manufacturers until 1884.			322
NOWLAN	See Shaw & Nowlan.			
NUTT	W. R. Nutt & Co., 39-43 Suffolk Road, 1894-1901. Nutt took over the premises of the long established firm of Shaw & Fisher which closed down in 1894.			323

-O-

1	2	3	4	5
OATES	Daniel Oates, 88 Broad Lane, 1833; 11 Workhouse Lane, 1834-1841. Spoon maker.			324
	Oates & Hudson, Cutts Works, 41 Division St., 1868-1869.			325
	Thomas Oates, 46 Burgess St. and 104 Carver St., 1870-1876.			326
OLDHAM	Oldham & Sewell, 53 Arundel St., 1864-1876.			327
	James Oldham, 69 Arundel St., c. 1877-c. 1894.			328
	James Oldham & Co., 9 Eyre Lane, 1895-1897; Surry Lane, 1989-1900.			329
ORFORD	Orford & Co., Surry Plate Works, Surry Lane, 1931-1933.			330

1	2	3	4	5
OSBALDISTON	H. Osbaldiston & Sons, 92 Arundel St., 1884.			331
OSBORNE	William Osborne, 83 Back-fields, 1907-1908.			332
	Osborne & Co., 82 Backfields, 1909-1911; 122 Rockingham, 1912-1916; 207 Rockingham, 1917-1939. The firm became a limited company in 1928. Osborne, an electroplate manufacturer, registered the name Abbey in 1913 for use on plated wares. Pewter wares were added about 1920 and the use of the mark on those wares would date from that year.	*Abbey* PEWTER HAND HAMMERED	c.1920-1939	333
OTLEY	John and Thomas Otley, 54 Eyre St., 1830-c. 1832.			334
	Richard and Thomas Otley, Union Place, 1833-1836; Trafalgar St., 1837-c. 1845.	T OTLEY SHEFFIELD	1833-c. 1845	335
	Thomas Otley & Co., Lambert Place, c. 1846-1860.	R & T OTLEY SHEFFIELD	c.1845-1860	336
	Thomas Otley, Lambert Place, 1861-1862; 33 Meadow St., 1863-1872; New Meadow St., 1873-1875.	THOMAS OTLEY SHEFFIELD	1861-1875	337
	Thomas Otley & Sons, New Meadow St., 1876-1922. The trade mark appeared first in 1889. The firm became limited in 1900. Many of their wares were electroplated.	THOMAS OTLEY & SONS SHEFFIELD	1876-1888	338
		THOMAS OTLEY & SONS SHEFFIELD	1889-c. 1900	339
		THOMAS OTLEY & SONS SHEFFIELD	1889-c. 1900	340
	Thomas Otley & Son, 9 Eyre Lane, 1908-1910.			341
	Thomas Otley & Sons, 9 Eyre Lane, 1911-1933. Whereas the earlier Otley firm (1876-1922) engaged in the manufacture			342

1	2	3	4	5
OTLEY (cont')	of Britannia metal and plated goods, the second firm (1908-1933) supplied to the trade for electroplating.			
	William Otley & Co., 69 Henry St., 1893.			343
OWEN	Owen & Levick, 92 Wellington, 1852-1853.			344
	Charles Owen, 92 Wellington, 1854-1855; 130 West St., 1856-1860; Eldon St., 1861-1862.			345
	Charles Owen & Co., 7 Eldon St., 1863-1875; 12 Baker's Hill, 1876-1883; 111 Arundel St., 1884-1886; 48 Button Lane, 1887-1891.			346
	Robert Owen, 58 Allen St., 1876.			347
	Denison Owen, Victoria Mills, Corporation St., 1879-1884.			348
	Owen Brothers, 12 Baker's Hill, 1879-1887.			349
	James Owen, 13 Baker's Hill, 1884.			350
	Also see Froggatt & Owen.			
OXLEY	See Land & Oxley.			
	-P-			
PALLETT	See Dawson & Pallett.			
PARAMORE	See Flanagan & Paramore.			
PARK	See John Batt.			
PARKER	Joseph Parker, Alexander Works, 91 Arundel and 58 Trinity St., 1876-1877.			351
	Joseph Parker & Sons, 58-60 Trinity St., 1878-1883; 50 Trinity St., 1884.			352
PARKIN	Wm. Parkin, 53 Campo Lane, 1812-1821; 6 Campo Lane, 1822-1824; 46 Campo Lane, 1825-1827; 42 Campo Lane, 1828-1833.	PARKIN	1812-1833	353
	John Parkin, 20 Bridge St., 1830.			354
	Thomas & Richard Parkin, Campo Lane, 1834-1835.	R.&T. PARKIN	1834-1835	355

1	2	3	4	5
PARKIN (cont')	Thomas Parkin, 42 Campo Lane, 1836-1838; 15 Sycamore, 1839-1871; Sidney St., 1872.	T. PARKIN SHEFFIELD	1836-1838	356
		V [crown] R T. PARKIN SHEFFIELD	1837-1838	357
		THOS. PARKIN 15 SYCAMORE ST. SHEFFIELD	1839-1871	358
	Richard Parkin, 4 Hawley Croft, c. 1836-1844; 40 Campo Lane, 1845-1852.			359
	R. (Richard) Parkin & Son, 40 Campo Lane, 1853-1858; 30 Pond Hill, 1859-1872.	V [crown] R RICHARD PARKIN & SON SHEFFIELD	1853-1872	360
	Parkin & Marshall, Furnival St., 1861-1862.			361
	E. H. Parkin & Co. (Parkin Silversmiths, Ltd. from 1977). The firm was founded in May, 1919, as E. H. Parkin & Co. 212 Brook Hill 1919-1929 122 Scotland St. 1930-1953 124 Scotland St. 1954-1977 Bowling Green St. 1977++ In July, 1977 the name changed to Parkin Silversmiths, Ltd. and the company moved to new premises at Cornwall Works, Bowling Green Street. The cameo in a large oval was used from 1925 to 1965. From 1965 the company initials and a small cameo appear in 4 small shields. In 1977, the initials changed to reflect the new name of the firm. In 1952, Parkin took over the old firm of T. Land & Son, Ltd. and continued their trade mark, CIVIC, until 1977. Trade marks for the American market included CHELTENHAM and GENTRY.	[oval] CAMEO PEWTER	1925-1965	362
		E H P [shields]	1965-1977	363
		[crest] CHELTENHAM AND COMPANY MADE IN SHEFFIELD ENGLAND	1946-1955	364
		[crown] EC GENTRY	1955-1975	365
		P S L [shields]	1977++	366
PATTEN	George Patten, Coalpit Lane. White metal framed cutlery, c. 1785-c. 1800.	[cross] PATEN	c. 1785-c. 1800	367
	Hannah Patten & Son, Silver St., c. 1785-c. 1803. This cutlery firm was listed in the 1787 directory as makers of knives framed in white metal and in the 1797 directory as pen knife cutlers. It may be presumed that some pen knife styles were framed in white metal. The address given the 1797 is 42 Silver Street, the same	[cross] NANTZ	c. 1785-c. 1803	368

1	2	3	4	5
PATTEN (cont')	premises where James Dixon established his business about 1804.			
PEARCE	John Pearce, 15 Angel St., 1836-1839; 38 Angel St., 1840-1852. Spoons were a specialty during the early years.	I. PEARCE 15 ANGEL ST	1836-1839	369
		I. PEARCE SHEFFIELD	1840-1852	370
PEARSON	S. Pearson & Co., 107 Eldon, 1854.			371
	Thomas Pearson, Pool Works, Burgess St., 1905-1908.			372
PERIOD	See Frank Cobb & Co.			
PETFIELD	Petfield, Harrison & Wilson, Havelock Works, Walker St., 1876.			373
	Jackson Petfield, Nursery Wheel, Stanley St., 1876.			374
PMC	The Pewter Manufacturing Co. (PMC) was organized in 1968 by Alan Aikin and serves as a prime example of a modern pewter works. Their sole product is pewter and although tankards are the main items produced, a complete line of wares is manufactured. Goods are exported world wide under a variety of trade marks including KENT, LEONARD and EALES. Wares are also made for numerous other firms whose names are placed on the goods.	ENGLISH PEWTER MADE IN SHEFFIELD ENGLAND	1970++	375
			1970++	376
			1970++	377
PHOENIX	See Hall & Phoenix.			
PINDER	Pinder Brothers, 48 Garden St. Primarily electroplated wares, 1895++. Pewter wares date from 1963 and are made for Pinder Bros. by Arundel Stainless Ware and James Lodge, both owned by Pinder's. The Pinder logo has been in use since 1963.	PINDER BROS. ENGLISH PEWTER SHEFFIELD	1963++	378
			1963++	379
PLANT	James Plant, 154 Fitzwilliam St., c. 1865. Flask maker.			380
PLATTS	Joseph Platts & Co., 60 Broomhall St.			381
POTTER	John Henry Potter, 124 Rockingham, 1884-1890; 65 Division St., 1891-1938.			382

1	2	3	4	5
	-Q- No entries.			
	-R-			
RAND	See Roberts & Dore			
RATCLIFFE	George Ratcliffe, 12 Love St., 1841.			383
	R. (Rowland) Ratcliffe & Sons, London Works, Bridge St., 1876-1884.			384
REANEY	Reaney, Lee & Co., Eldon St., 1871-1872.			385
REDFEARN	Thomas Redfearn, 65 Coalpit Lane, 1845, Spoon maker.			386
RELIABLE	See Sheffield Plate Co.; Alfred R. Ecroyd; Bramwell, Brownhill & Co.			
RICHARDSON	Richard Richardson, Cornwall Works, Pond Hill, 1873-1883; 167 Norfolk St., 1884-1890; Scotland St., 1891-1925. In 1889 Richardson had taken over the John Harrison firm. Richardson became a limited company in 1910 and produced only electroplated wares from 1912.	R.RICHARDSON CORNWALL WORKS SHEFFIELD	1873-c. 1900	387
	Also see Southern & Richardson.			
RIDGE	Ridge, Woodcock & Hardy, 143 Eldon St., 1876-1880. The trade mark was continued by Woodcock & Hardy (q.v.) from 1881 to 1895.		1876-1895	388
	Joseph Ridge & Co., Lion Works, 47 Eyre Lane, 1880-1884.	JOSEPH RIDGE & CO SHEFFIELD	1880-1884	389
RILEY	Wm. Riley, although listed as a manufacturer, was primarily a merchant, 1841-1849.	W. RILEY SHEFFIELD	1841-1849	390
ROBERTS	Samuel Roberts, Jr. was a very prominent maker of Sheffield Plate who introduced many innovations to that industry which became standard procedure for many makers. In 1790 Roberts received patent No. 1722 for plating			

1	2	3	4	5
ROBERTS (cont')	silver over while metal (Britannia metal). The method was not a success due to the difficulty in construction of the wares, particularly in soldering. Some wares were made by the process and they occasionally show up on the antique market. A bell was the Sheffield Plate mark registered by Roberts (and Cadman) in 1785. It was also used by late 19th century electroplaters in England and America.			
	Roberts & Co., 7 Shoreham, 1859-1868.			391
	Roberts & Briggs, Furnival Works, 1862-1863.			392
	Roberts & Belk, Furnival Works, 38 Furnival St., 1864++.			393
	Roberts, Dore' & Hall, 4 Eyre Lane, 1910-1912.			394
	Roberts & Dore', Ltd., Sheffield and London, 1913++. The trade mark RAND has been in continuous use on pewter and electroplate wares from c. 1920. Also see Baines & Roberts	RAND	1920++	395
ROBINSON	Robinson & Kitchens (Kitching), South St., 1825-1829.			396
RODGERS	Joseph Rodgers & Sons Ltd. claimed origin in 1682. Although primarily a cutlery and silver firm, Britannia metal wares may have been produced. Mark No. 397 was given in the directory of 1787 as that used on their knives framed with white metal. At that time the firm was known as Joseph and Maurice Rodgers.	✳ ✠ RODGERS	c. 1787-c. 1800	397
		RODGERS	c. 1900-c. 1939	398
ROLLASON	A Rollason & Sons, 4 Surry St., 1887.			399
ROUND	John Round began in the electroplate trade and silver wares were their primary products. Pewter wares were produced under the trade name "HERALDIC" during the 1920's and 1930's. John Round, Tudor Works, Tudor St., 1852-1862;			400

1	2	3	4	5
ROUND (cont')	John Round & Son, Tudor Works, Tudor St., 1863-1875; John Round & Son, Ltd., Tudor Works, Tudor St., 1876-1934; John Round & Son, Ltd., Pond Hill, 1935-1957.			
ROWBOTHAM	See Wingfield, Rowbotham & Co.			
RUSSELL	Samuel Russell was a very active manufacturer in Sheffield. He worked with two different partnerships and on his own at two different periods. He especially advertised his "extra hard" metal and held two patents for unique handles. Samuel Russell, 188 West St., 1845-1851. From 1852 to 1860 Russell worked in the partnership of Buxton & Russell (q.v.).	SAM'L RUSSELL EXTRA HARD SHEFFIELD	1845-1851	401
	Russell & Travis, 76 Eyre St., 1861-1863. See G. Travis & Co.			402
	Samuel Russell, 20 Ellis St., 1864-1891.			403
	Also see Buxton & Russell.			
RUTHERFORD	Rutherford, Stacey, West & Co., Britannia Place, Garden St., 1836-1842. This firm succeeded John Vickers, son to James Vickers, originator of the industry. They used no mark of their own name but continued the use of I. Vickers (q.v.).			404

-S-

1	2	3	4	5
SAMPSON	Henry Sampson, 22 Orchard St., 1824-1828.			405
	Sampson, Wish & Co., 3 Paradise St., 1876.			406
	Also see Green, Sampson & Green; Green, Sampson & Co.			
SANDERS	John Sanders, Gate Yard, 1828-1829. Spoon maker.			407
SEWELL	See Oldham & Sewell.			
SHACKLETON	See Wardle & Shackleton.			
SHALLCROSS	Wm. Shallcross, 1845. Spoon maker.			408

1	2	3	4	5
SHARMAN	Sharman & Hydes, Cyprus Works, Fawcett St., 1879.			409
	Edwin Sharman, Cyprus Works, Daisy Walk, 1880-1884.			410
SHAW	George Shaw & Co., 25 Allen St., 1820-1823.			411
	George Shaw & Son, Allen St., 1824-1826.			412
	George & James Shaw, Killham's Wheel, 1827-1828.			413
	George Shaw, Brocco, 1829-1832; 28 Allen St., 1833-1838; 56 Osborne, 1839-c. 1845; 147 Allen, c. 1845-1858.			414
	George Shaw & Co., 147 Allen, 1859-1864.			415
	James Shaw, Kellham Works, 1829-1830. (A dissolution of George & James Shaw). (q.v.)			416
	(James) Shaw & Fisher, Kellham Works, 1830-1836; 14 Howard Place, 1837-1844; 43 Suffolk Road, 1845-1894. Mark No. 418 is reduced for inclusion here.	SHAW & FISHER SHEFFIELD	1833-1872	417
			1844-c. 1854	418
		SHAW & FISHER SHEFFIELD	1872-1894	419
		SHAW & FISHER 43 SUFFOLK RD. SHEFFIELD	1872-1894	420
	W. Shaw, 174 Broomhall, 1961-1962.			421
	Shaw & Nowland, Howard Works, Broad St., 1963-1966.			422
	Wm. Shaw Ltd., Howard Works, Broad St., 1967-1971.			423

1	2	3	4	5
SHEFFIELD	Sheffield Plate Manufacturing Co., Ltd., 48 Robert St., 1884. This short lived firm originated the *Reliable* trade mark which was taken over by Alfred R. Ecroyd in 1884 (q.v.). The mark was later revised when taken over by Bramwell, Brownhill & Co. in 1891.			424
SHELDON	Wm. Henry Sheldon, 150 Rockingham Lane, 1896-1935.			425
	Wm. Henry Sheldon & Son, 188 Solly St., 1912-1935.			426
SHEPHERD	See Marshes & Shepherd.			
SIMPSON	John Simpson, Scotland St., 1828-1830. Spoon maker.			427
SKINNER	Skinner, Coulson & Branson, 1854.			428
	Skinner & Branson, 17 Sycamore St., 1855-1859.	SKINNER & CO. PATENTEES SHEFFIELD	1855-1859	429
	Thomas Skinner, 7 Eldon St., 1860; 29 Charlotte St., 1861-1863; Eldon St., 1864.			430
SLACK	Slack Brothers, 17 Leicester St., 1864.			431
SLATER	Slater Brothers, 94 Scotland St., 1884.			432
SMITH	George & James Smith, Allen St., 1812-1815.			433
	George Smith, Allen St., 1816-1817.			434
	William Smith & Co., Coalpit Lane was listed in the 1787 and 1797 directories as makers of knives framed in white metal.	IES	1787-c. 1800	435
	Also see Briggs & Smith; Dixon & Smith; Kirkby, Smith & Co.			

1	2	3	4	5
SOUTHERN	Southern & Richardson, Don Cutlery Works, Doncaster St. Established in 1863 as a cutlery firm, a more complete line of wares, primarily electroplated, were added from 1887.	SOUTHERN & RICHARDSON SHEFFIELD	1887-c. 1900	436
STACEY	John Stacey, Radford Place, 1839.			437
	E. (Ebenezer) Stacey, a nephew to John Vickers, was a partner in Rutherford, Stacey, West & Co., which took over I. Vickers upon the retirement of John Vickers in 1836. In 1843, the firm assumed his name, and the mark included the phrase "successor to I. Vickers."			
	E. Stacey, 40 Garden St., 1843-1856.	E. STACEY SUCCESSOR TO I. VICKERS BRITANNIA PLACE SHEFFIELD	1843-1856	438
	E. Stacey & Son, Garden St., 1857-1920; (Hodges Brothers, 20 Fitzwilliams St., Proprietors, 1921-1934.) Primarily electroplated wares in the 20th century.	E. STACEY & SON SUCCESSORS TO JOHN VICKERS BRITANNIA PLACE SHEFFIELD	1857-c. 1900	439
		E. STACEY & SONS SHEFFIELD	c. 1870-c. 1900	440
	G. H. Stacey & Co., Exchange Works, West St., 1876.			441
	Also see Rutherford, Stacey, West & Co.			
STANDISH	See Armitages & Standish.			
STANIFORTH	Padley Staniforth & Co., Hartshead, 1856-1868.			442
	Also see Deakin & Staniforth.			
STEVENSON	J & J Stevenson, 4 Furnival Lane, 1841-1845. Spoon maker.			443
	-T-			
TALBOT	See Thomas Turner.			
TATEHAM	Edmund Tateham, 32 Harrow St., 1898-1902.			444
TAYLOR	Wm. Taylor was neither a maker nor from Sheffield. His name occasionally appears on wares made by Arthur E. Furniss.			445

1	2	3	4	5
THOMPSON	Joseph Thompson, 185 South St., 1859.			446
TOOTHILL	Robert Toothill, 20 Bower Spring, 1849-1862.			447
	M. Toothill, 18 Princess St., 1861-1862.			448
TOWNROE	Townroe & Sons, West Bar, 1862-1962. From 1865 the firm is described as "finishers to the trade". Primarily electroplating service for other makers.	TOWNROE & SONS WEST BAR SHEFFIELD	1862-c. 1865	449
TOWNSEND	Francis J. (John) Townsend, 214 Solly St., 1876-1903.			450
TRAFALGAR	See Harrison Fisher.			
TRAVIS	George Travis began in partnership with Samuel Russell in 1861. In 1863 they separated, each with his own company. G. Travis & Co. was established in that year at 69 Charles St. In 1868 a move was made to Clarance Works, 13 Bath St. In 1909, the firm became Travis, Wilson & Co. (q.v.).			451
	Travis, Wilson & Co., Ltd., was the continuation of G. Travis & Co. and dates from 1909 at the Clarance Works, 13 Bath St. In 1967, a move was made to 85 Denby St. In 1926, the firm took over the trade name of MANOR PEWTER from A Milns for their own- MANOR PERIOD PEWTER. The Travis, Wilson firm serves as a good example of one of many Sheffield firms which produced wares under trade description of Britannia Metal in the 19th century and then produced the same wares in the 20th century under the trade description of Sheffield Pewter. The firm was taken over by Julius Isaacs in 1967.	MANOR PERIOD T.W. & Co. LTD SHEFFIELD PEWTER	1926-1939	452
	Also see Russell & Travis.			
TURNER	Charles Turner, Nursery Lane, 1858-1859.			453
	Turner & Bramwell, Nursery Lane, 1860.			454
	Samuel Turner, China Square in 1787 and Howard St. in 1797, was a maker of knives framed in white metal.	IVORY	1787-c. 1800	455

1	2	3	4	5
TURNER (cont')	Thomas Turner & Co., Suffolk Rd., 1886-1937. This firm which manufactured silver wares, produced pewter goods under the trade name of TALBOT during the 1920's and 1930's.			456
	Wm. Turner, 47 Rockingham Lane, 1829-1834.			457
TYAS	F. A. Tyas & Co., 14 Sycamore St., 1954++.			458
	Also see Gordon & Tyas.			
TYLER	I. (John) Tyler was one of those who held to the custom of using the old I for the initial J. Walker St., 1836-1839; 9 Andrew St., 1840-1844; 17 Joiner Lane, 1845-1853; 52 Stanley, 1854-1855; 17 Joiner, 1856-1859; Johnson Lane, 1860; Tomcross Lane, 1861-1864; 1 Brunswick Road, 1865-1869.	I. TYLER SHEFFIELD	1836-1869	459
	William Tyler (successor to I. Tyler), Brunswick Road, 1869-1882.			460
	William Tyler & Sons, Brunswick Road, 1882-1928.			461
	Also see Brown, Tyler & Brown.			
TYSACK	Mark Tysack & Son, 92 Carver St., 1848-1865. Spoon and parts maker.			462
	Mark Tysack & Sons, 29 Westfield Terrace, 1866-1869. Parts maker to the trade.			463
	-U-			
UNION	Union Co., Steelhouse Lane, 1830.			464
UNITY	Unity was the trade mark used by the Cooperative Wholesale Society for pewter wares made for them by Barker Brothers of Birmingham during the 1920's and 1930's.	"UNITY" PEWTER	c. 1925-1939	465

1	2	3	4	5
	-V-			
VICKERS	James Vickers was the originator of the white metal-Britannia metal-pewter industry that continues to flourish in present day Sheffield. His addresses were: Hollis St., 1769-1774; Hartshead, 1775-1776; Sims Croft, 1777; Campo Lane, 1778; Broad Lane, 1778-1787; Garden Walk (St.), 1787-1842. Vickers died in 1809, and the firm continued under the direction of his son, John. In 1836 John Vickers sold the firm to Rutherford, Stacey, West & Co. Ebenezer Stacey was John Vickers' nephew. During the six years under the organization of Rutherford, Stacey, West & Co., 1836-1842, the Vickers' name continued in use with the addition of either "Britannia Place", or the city name "Sheffield". In 1843, Stacey took over the firm and used his own name and mark. Attention has been drawn in previous publications to the variance in the size of the I. Vickers incised mark used from c. 1787 to 1836, with suggestions that wares could be dated by the size of the mark. It should be noted that the size has no significance. Over a period of many years new and additional punches were made, accounting for the variety of sizes.	I✱VICKERS	1769-c. 1787	466
		I.VICKERS	c. 1787-1836	467
		I. VICKERS BRITANNIA PLACE	1836-1840	468
		I.VICKERS SHEFFIELD	1840-1842	469
VIENER	The firm currently producing electroplated wares in Sheffield was organized in 1908, by W & A Viener and the company names, addresses and dates are as follows: W & E Viener, 136 West St., 1908-1912; W & E Viener, 76 Bath St., 1913-1921; A & E Viener, 76 Bath St., 1922-1924; A & E Viener Ltd., 76 Bath St., 1925. Viner's Ltd., 76 Bath St., 1926 to the present. Pewter wares were produced under the trade name of CRAFTSMAN during the period 1926-1939. Variations in Mark No. 472 may occur.			470
		CRAFTSMAN PEWTER SHEFFIELD	c. 1926-1939	471
VINER'S		CRAFTSMAN SHEFFIELD PEWTER	c. 1926-1939	472

1	2	3	4	5
VINER'S (cont')		*Viners English Pewter Sheffield* MADE IN ENGLAND	1948-c. 1960	473
		VINERS of Sheffield English Pewter Made in England	c. 1960-c. 1974	474
	-W-			
WALKER	George Walker was an unemployed table knife forger in 1843 when the method of electroplating became a successful venture in Sheffield. The first practical, commercial license for electroplating was granted to John Harrison in Sheffield on June 13 1843. Harrison hired George Walker to go to Birmingham to learn the plating process from Elkington's, the inventors. Two years later, in 1845, George Walker, with a partner, Samuel Coulson, established the firm of Walker & Co. on Howard St. The firm made no wares of their own but plated wares manufactured by the other makers in Sheffield. In 1852 the company, reorganized as Walker & Hall, began producing their own wares and eventually became one of the largest silver manufacturers in the world. The use of the pennant as a trade mark began in 1861 and remained in use until Walker & Hall was taken over by British Silversmiths Ltd. in 1961. Walker & Hall, Howard St., 1852-1961.	W&H WALKER&HALL SHEFFIELD	1861-1890	475
		W&H WALKER&HALL SHEFFIELD ENGLAND	1891-1909	476
		W&H WALKER&HALL SHEFFIELD MADE IN ENGLAND	1910-1961	477
		HOWARD W&H W&H PEWTER WALKER & HALL SHEFFIELD MADE IN ENGLAND	c. 1930-1939	478
		REGISTERED TRADE MARK Homestead ENGLISH PEWTER HAND BEATEN	c. 1920-c. 1930	479

1	2	3	4	5
WALKER (cont')	Walker & Co., 106 St. Mary's St., 1907-1912; 21 Cambridge St., 1913-1918; 91 Button St., 1919-1935. Walker & Co. became a limited company in 1924 and produced electro-plated wares. Pewter wares were produced from 1930-1935 under the trade mark of HOMELAND.	HOMELAND	1930-1935	480
WALKLAND	I. (James) Walkland & Co., 124 West Bar, 1865-1868; Lambert St., 1869-1875; Orchard Lane, 1876. Design registrations for 1869 and 1870 are registered in the name of Calvert, Walkland & Co.			481
WALTON	T. Walton & Co., 1 Court, Scotland St., c. 1865. Also see Jackson & Walton.			482
WARBURTON	Sam Warburton, 62 Hollis Croft, 1821; 55 Trippet Lane, 1822-1832; 6 Broad Lane, 1833-1834.			483
	Samuel & Henry Warburton, Hollis St., 1830.			484
	Eliz. Warburton, 116 South St., 1859-1860.			485
WARDLE	Wardle & Shackleton, 13 Upper Hanover St., 1948.			486
	Wardle & Matthews, Randall St., 1965++. Wares are produced under the trade name of NOBLEMAN.	MADE IN ENGLAND BY WARDLE & MATTHEWS	1965++	487
		FINE ENGLISH PEWTER	1965++	488
			1965+	489
WARNER	Charles Warner, 39 Eyre St., 1923-1924.			490
WATER	Godfrey Water & Son, Pond Lane was listed in the 1787 directory as makers of knives framed in white metal.	WATER	c. 1787	491
WEBSTER	Webster & Johnson's, 4 Sycamore St., c. 1840-c. 1845.	V R WEBSTER & JOHNSON'S	c. 1840-c. 1845	492

254

1	2	3	4	5
WENTWORTH	A. R. Wentworth, 104 West St., 1948++.	*English Pewter by A. R. Wentworth of Sheffield*	1948++	493
		MADE IN ENGLAND	1948++	494
		BROOKS BROTHERS MADE IN ENGLAND	1948++	495
WEST	See Rutherford, Stacey, West & Co.			
WHITE	John White, 19 Pond St., 1856.			496
	R. Sutcliffe White, 127 Fitzwilliam St., 1871.			497
	Also see Lee, White & Co.; Nicholson & White.			
WHITEHEAD	Henry Cox Whitehead, 80 Bowden St., 1896-1900.			498
	Mrs. Annie Whitehead, Arundel Works, Eyre Lane, 1904-1905.			499
WIGFULL	See Lee & Wigfull.			
WILKINS	See Marples, Wingfield & Wilkins.			
WILKINSON	Henry Wilkinson worked in the silver and Old Sheffield Plate trade from 1828 but did not enter the Britannia metal trade until 1843. 46 Castle Mills, 1843-1853; 13 Wicker Lane, 1854-1858; 167 South St., 1859; Wicker Lane, 1860; Great Green Lane, 1861-1863; 13 Eyre Lane, 1864-1890; Division St., 1891.	WILKINSON	1843-c. 1860	500
	T. (Thomas) Wilkinson, Kenyon Alley, 223 Allen St., 1868-1875; New Edward St. and Kenyon Alley, Allen St., 1876-1880; 95 Edward St., 1881.			501
	Frederick William Wilkinson, Orchard Works, Orchard Lane, 1883-1884.			502
	Wilkinson Brothers, Arundel Works, Howard Lane, 1884-1888, Eyre St., 1889-1903; Boston St., 1904-1910.			503

1	2	3	4	5
WILSON	John Wilson, Brinsworths Orchard, was listed in the 1787 directory as a maker of knives framed in white metal.	BILBOA	c. 1787	504
	Joseph Wilson of Carver St. was listed in the 1787 directory as a maker of knives framed in white metal.	IDEA	c. 1787	505
	Samuel Wilson, Trippet Lane, c. 1810-1820. Spoon maker.			506
	Sarah Wilson & Son, Widow and son (Samuel Jr.) of Samuel Wilson. 64 Trippet Lane, 1821-1827; Union Lane at the top of Charles St., 1828-1838. Spoon makers.			507
	Samuel Wilson, the younger, 152 Solly St., 1839-1841.			508
	F. Wilson & Co., 9-13 Cavendish St., 1889.			509
	Also see Methley & Wilson; Petfield, Harrison & Wilson.			
WINGFIELD	Wingfield, Rowbotham & Co., Suffolk Road, 1911-1928. Upon the close of this firm, Wingfield took an interest in George Lee & Co. (q.v.).			510
WISH	George Wish, Denmark Works, Norfolk Lane, 1879-1887.			511
	Also see Sampson. Wish & Co.			
WITHERS	Benjamin Withers & Co., Fargate, was a maker of cutlery framed in white metal. c. 1787-1793.	ESPANGE	c. 1787-1793	512
WOLSTENHOLME	Samuel & Joseph Wolstenholme, Spring St., 1822-1823. This firm began in 1821 as Miller & Wolstenholme (q.v.).			513
	Joseph Wolstenholme, Spring St., 1824-1827; 10 Broad St., 1828-1857.	I. WOLSTENHOLME	c. 1824	514
		· J. WOLSTENHOLME · SHEFFIELD	1824-1857	515
	W. F. Wolstenholme, 31 Broad St., 1858-1860; Stanley Lane, Wicker, 1861-1870.			516
	Wolstenholme, Maclaurin & Co., 117 Matilda, 1871-1875.			517

1	2	3	4	5
WOLSTENHOLME (cont')	Wolstenholme & Biggin, Matilda St., 1876-1879. (See Henry Biggin.)	WOLSTENHOLME & BIGGIN 117 MATILDA STREET SHEFFIELD	1876-1879	518
	W. Wolstenholme & Son, Ecclesall Works, 144 Rockingham Lane, 1880-1895.			519
	Also see Miller & Wolstenholme.			
WOODCOCK	John Woodcock, 12 Grindlegate, 1830.			520
	Woodcock & Hardy, Eldon Place, 145 Eldon St., 1881-1895. The trade mark "XTRA" dates from registration of the mark by Ridge, Woodcock & Hardy in 1876 (q.v.).		1876-1895	521
	Thomas Woodcock & Sons. Woodcock took over the old Shaw & Fisher premises from W. R. Nutt & Co., (q.v.), 43 Suffolk Road, 1908-1930; 90 Eyre Lane, 1930-1957.			522

-X-

No entries.

-Y-

No entries.

-Z-

No entries.

INDEX
(Also see Chapter VIII)